An Introduction to
TAROT

Cassandra Bee

CHARTWELL
BOOKS, INC.

Published in 2008 by
CHARTWELL BOOKS, INC.
A division of BOOK SALES, INC.
114 Northfield Avenue
Edison, New Jersey 08837
USA

**Copyright © 2008 Regency
House Publishing Limited**
Niall House
24–26 Boulton Road
Stevenage, Hertfordshire
SG1 4QX, UK

For all editorial enquiries please contact
Regency House Publishing at
www.regencyhousepublishing.com

ISBN-13: 978-0-7858-2402-2

ISBN-10: 0-7858-2402-2

Printed in China

CAUTION: Tarot is a fascinating subject,
not least because of its long and interesting
history. Many people down the ages have
ascribed divinatory powers to the cards,
while just as many see them as a form of
entertainment. The information in this
book has been written and should be used
only with good intentions in mind, and
must on no account be used in a negative or
harmful way.

CONTENTS

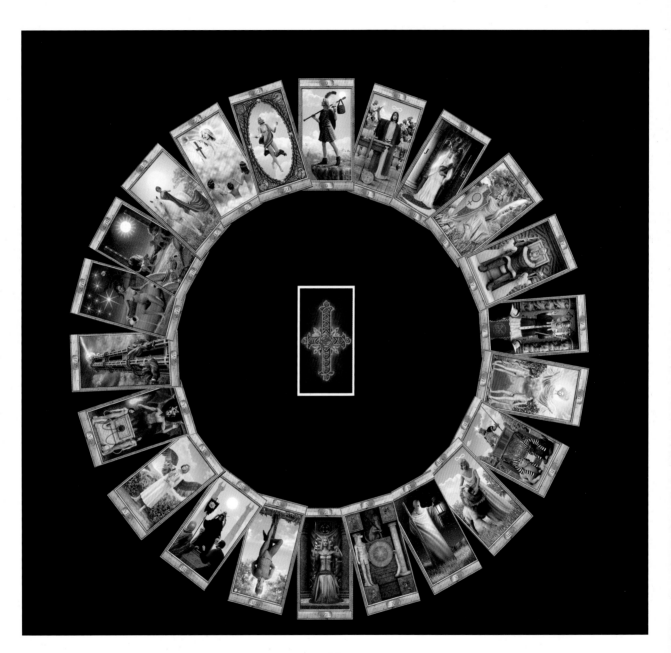

Dear Reader,

The Tarot is a medieval system of divination and esoteric knowledge that was developed in Europe and went on to become one of the most popular systems of self-discovery and future-prediction in the world. You will find that working with the Tarot's 78 cards will prove to be a source of constant amazement.

The cards combine symbolic representations of the basic truths of life with more arcane references to ancient wisdom and philosophy. Therefore, it's always important to remember that although the cards can be used as predictive tools, the best Tarot readers will always favour interpretations that empower people rather than foretell outcomes. Good Tarot readers understand the adage, 'Wisdom is best used subtly'.

This book will guide you through the 22 Major Arcana and the 56 Minor Arcana cards separately, before they are used in combination in the chapter, Putting It Together, which contains some initial thoughts to get you started. Once you've begun your own journey through the Tarot, you may decide to formulate your own interpretations, based on your experiences, on your own understanding of the archetypes, and on numerology, colour-wisdom and so on.

Understanding the Tarot is a lifelong journey that ultimately leads to great enlightenment.

I wish you the best of luck and true inspiration as you prepare to travel along this path.

With love,

Cassandra Bee

CHAPTER ONE

HISTORY OF THE TAROT

The true origins of the Tarot were lost to myth and romanticism a long time ago, but not before scholars, occultists and esotericists had tried to make it suit their own purposes. Playing cards were originally the invention of the Chinese, but the type that appeared in Europe in the late 1300s, with suits of scimitars, polo sticks, cups and coins, is attributed to the Egyptian Mamelukes, evolving into the basic Latin suits of swords, wands, cups and pentacles.

The first European Tarot decks were created between 1410 and 1430 in northern Italy, being a combination of the original four-suited set of playing cards to which an additional 22 trump cards, known as *carte di trionfi* and illustrated with allegorical figures, were added. Of these Tarot sets, the oldest surviving is the *Tarocchi* of Bonifacio Bembo, created in the mid-15th century for the powerful Visconti-Sforza family of Milan.

Medieval and Renaissance society appears to have been receptive to influences of all kinds, especially the esoteric traditions, and members of the

artistocracy liked to dabble in all manner of new foreign 'diversions'. It is reasonable to suppose, therefore, that references to esoteric practices would have lain deeply buried in Bembo's Tarot that it would have been wise to keep to oneself if the wrath of the Christian church was to be avoided. Because of its outwardly harmless appearance as a popular gaming system, therefore, the Tarot escaped attempts at driving hermetic and non-Christian influences out of Europe. But we must remember that the Renaissance marked the beginning of artistic innovation as well as

LEFT: Some believe the Tarot originated in ancient Egypt, in that the name is thought to have come from that of Thoth, the god of writing and esoteric knowledge.

OPPOSITE: Throughout the centuries, cards have been used for game-playing, cartomancy and divination.

the famous French *Tarot de Marseille*, that would go through something of a renaissance of its own, when it became the standard from which many Tarot decks of the 19th century and later were derived.

LEFT: Aritmetrica, *from the Tarocchi del Mantegna, a classic series of 15th-century Venetian engravings.*

BELOW: The Tarocchi del Minchiate originated in 15th-century Florence.

religious turmoil, resulting in the huge social, spiritual and philosophical changes that were spreading like wildfire throughout Europe.

Dr. John Dee, a powerful member of Queen Elizabeth I's court, is known to have used the cards in conjunction with astrology to acquire esoteric knowledge. During this time, various decks came into common use, not least

No one knows when the Tarot first came to be used for divination, but fortune-telling, using similar cards existed as early as 1540. In 1781, Antoine Court de Gébelin wrote a history of the Tarot, claiming that the mysteries of Isis and Thoth lay hidden within it, the knowledge having been found in a volume, rescued when the Great Library of Alexandria mysteriously burned down. This may or may not be true, but it indicates a widespread tendency to become seduced by the kind of arcane orientalism that attaches itself to texts or symbols of great emotional or spiritual power. That said, it would be

BELOW LEFT: The Devil card is associated with the Earth and the zodiac sign of Capricorn. It represents our attachment to material things.

BELOW: John Dee, Elizabeth I's mathematician, astronomer, astrologer, geographer and occultist.

foolish to ignore or undermine this understandable form of mythmaking.

Myth is the means by which profound truths concerning the origins of mankind are conveyed. Myth is the language of the soul, whereas fact describes the material world. This wisdom is embodied in the 78 cards of the Tarot, of which the 22 cards of the Major Arcana are at its heart. Each symbolizes the powerful archetypes attached to people, spiritual states, virtues and circumstances common to humanity as a whole. The four suits making up the 56 cards of the Minor Arcana are an approximation to ordinary playing cards and tell of day-to-day situations, issues, struggles and occurrences.

Of the playing cards in use today, The Fool, which over time became known as 'the joker' or the 'wild card', is the only member of the Major Arcana to have survived in this form. The others have fallen out of common

OPPOSITE: Making a reading from a copy of the ancient Sforza-Visconti deck.

RIGHT: A copy of the French Tarot de Marseille.

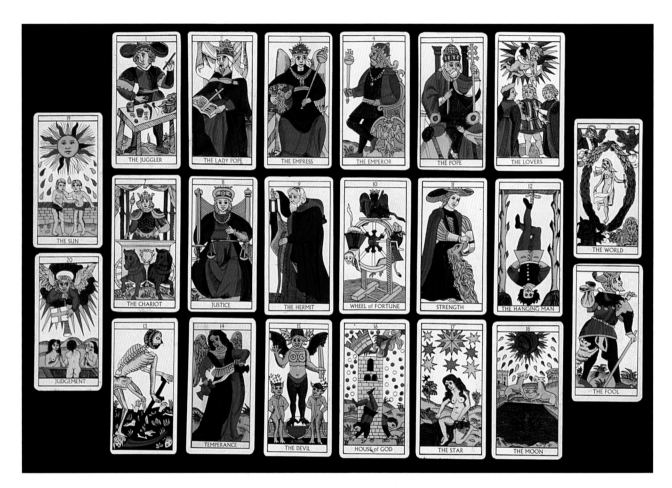

The 22 Major Arcana of the Tarot de Marseille deck.

usage and are now associated only with the esoteric Tarot.

The Tarot enjoyed something of a revival in the 19th century in the hands of esotericists such as Eliphas Lévi, when he linked the Tarot with a Hebrew 'Enochian alphabet', an occult or angelic language which had also been used in the private journals of Dr. John Dee and his seer, Edward Kelley, in the late 16th century. Lévi was a French priest and Rosicrucian who believed the Tarot to be the key to the Bible, the Jewish Kabbala and other ancient spiritual writings. He claimed there were parallels between the Tarot suits and the Tetragrammaton, the four letters of God's hidden name.

In 1910 the Rider-Waite Tarot deck was created, its images produced by the artist, Pamela Colman Smith, to the instructions of academic and mystic, A.E. Waite. It was published by the Rider Company and it is the deck on which the version that predominates in this book is based and which, according to Waite, restored true meaning to the Tarot.

Waite, a keen member of Aleister Crowley's Hermetic Order of the Golden Dawn, kept the images of his Tarot deceptively simple, even though they were packed with symbolism. Significantly, he altered the Christian imagery of older Tarot decks, turning the 'Pope' into the 'Hierophant' and the 'Popess' into the 'High Priestess', and controversially changed the order of the original sequence of the Major Arcana, based on his own understanding of esoteric traditions.

In 1940 Aleister Crowley and Lady Frieda Harris created their own deck,

based on Crowley's teachings. Crowley himself was a notorious figure, associated with the revival and re-popularization of magic in the 20th century. His book, *Magick in Theory and Practice*, which fuses Indian mysticism with his own style of Western magic, was the subject of much criticism. Together, Crowley and Harris undertook the long task of completely reworking the images of the Tarot to include their own magical symbols and practices, the intention being to enhance the practitioner's 'natural power'. Crowley is reported to have been suffering from deep depression when he was burned to death at his home in 1947. His cards, however, have become extremely widespread and are now second only in popularity to the Rider-Waite deck.

Whatever its origins, the Tarot has come to occupy an important position in Western esoteric tradition, in that penetrating insights can be gained from its pictorial content. It has been suggested that all humanity is united by a 'collective unconscious', which is a term used in analytical psychology, originally coined by Carl Jung. Jung distinguished the collective

unconscious from the personal unconscious that is unique to each human being, the collective being the 'reservoir of the experiences of our species' as a whole. Such archetypes are the stuff from which myth and legend are made, and appear in such characters as The Magician, The Hermit, The Empress. These are recognized by all of us on one level or another, regardless of time and place.

Eliphas Lévi, the French occultist and magician .

Such archetypes are the unconscious forces governing our lives which, once revealed, have the power to create profound inner change. The mystery that is inherent in the cards can only add to its appeal, while leading us to greater wisdom and enlightenment through self-knowledge.

ABOVE: Aleister Crowley, occultist and magician.

LEFT: Some of the Rider-Waite Major Arcana.

OPPOSITE LEFT: The Devil, from Aleister Crowley and Frieda Harris's Thoth deck.

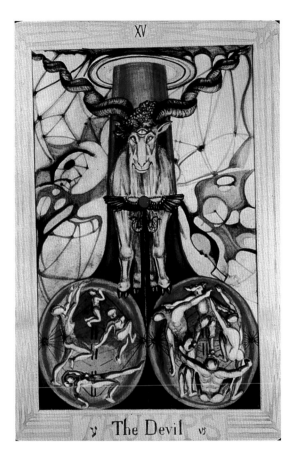

RIGHT: Part of Frieda Harris's illustration for the Knight of Cups.

PAGE 32: A reader using the Thoth deck.

PAGE 33: Other means of divination, including a crystal ball, used for scrying, and runestones.

29

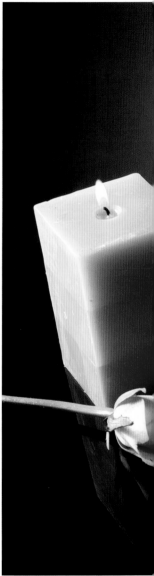

CHAPTER TWO

THE MAJOR ARCANA

Working with the Tarot's Major Arcana, the 'great secrets', is a profound experience, in that the 22 cards of this important set are reflections of the processes taking place on an inner level, rather than in the outer world of our daily lives. Therefore they are used less as divinatory tools and more as psychological or spiritual lessons, that point us towards the path whereby gnosis or inner wisdom may be achieved. However, the first card of the Major Arcana does not begin where we would expect it to, i.e. at number 1, but instead begins at 0. This is interesting because it makes us immediately aware that, although an important linear journey is about to be made through the major sequence (0–21), it also indicates a cyclical journey where the first card, 0, The Fool, is in direct proximity to the last card, 21, The World.

Circles and ovoids commonly appear in the language of esotericism. The 'cosmic egg' is found in the creation myths of many cultures and civilizations, and typically symbolizes the Universe, showing how all potentialities exist within one entity. The Fool bears the number zero, also resembling an egg, and The World is a woman surrounded by the same shape.

So although our journey through the Major Arcana can be made by reading the 22 cards along a straight line, we can also benefit from looking at them when they are arranged in a circular pattern.

Our circle begins and ends, therefore, with The Fool and The World lying side-by-side. If we compare the two lessons taught by the cards we see that the beginning and end of the journey mirror one another perfectly, each one illuminating something hidden from the other. If we continue to pair all the cards in the same way, ie. The Magician with Judgement; The High Priestess with

LEFT: The cosmic egg is a symbol of the Universe.

RIGHT: When the Major Arcana are arranged in a circle, the endless cycle of birth, death and rebirth is suggested.

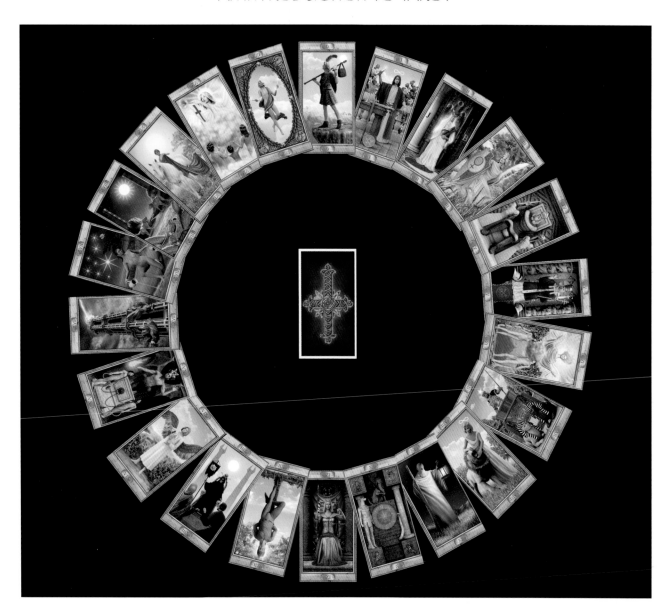

0 The Fool – XXI The World
I The Magician – XX Judgement
II The High Priestess – XIX The Sun
III The Empress – XVIII The Moon
IV The Emperor – XVII The Star
V The Hierophant – XVI The Tower
VI The Lovers – XV The Devil
VII The Chariot – XIV Temperance
VIII Strength – XIII Death
IX The Hermit – XII The Hanged Man
X The Wheel of Fortune – XI Justice

OPPOSITE & BELOW: Pairing the cards thus makes it simple to see what bearing one has on the other.

The Sun and so on *(see opposite)*, we find similar correspondences.

Another way to pair the cards is through a system of mirrored reflections *(see below)*. Beginning and ending with The Fool and The World, as before, we can therefore place the Major Arcana in two straight lines

(pairing I and XI, II and XII, III and XIII, etc.), each one of the pair saying something about the other. Compare the individual meanings of each pair and decide, when they are taken together, what it is they are teaching you. Try out both systems of pairing and see what you can learn from them. If you come to prefer one over the other, continue to use that one in future; once you have grown accustomed to that you may well wish to create a system of your own.

The Fool	The Magician	The High Priestess	The Empress	The Emperor	The Hierophant	The Lovers	The Chariot	Strength	The Hermit	The Wheel of Fortune
The World	Justice	The Hanged Man	Death	Temperance	The Devil	The Tower	The Star	The Moon	The Sun	Judgement

0. THE FOOL

The Fool sets out on his journey full of the joy and innocence of a child. He wears bright clothes and has a large red plume in his hat. He seems to be excitedly surveying the world around him, while surrounding him are the snowy tops of a mountain range. He stands at the edge of a precipice, with a white rose in his left hand and his travelling stick and bag in his right, blissfully unaware he is on the brink and may soon fall. Perhaps he is aware and simply doesn't care. He is prepared to make this great leap of faith. The Fool, in many ways, is divorced from time and space. His trust is so great that if he were to take the next step off the cliff we could imagine him magically walking across the sky supported by an invisible bridge.

The white rose in his hand indicates his innocence, which has a magical quality that makes it so total that it leads him to believe that anything he dreams up is bound to happen. On an inner level, The Fool represents the mystical traveller within us all, whose goal it is to seek out wisdom itself. Numerologically, his number is zero, signifying his journey has no beginning and no

Zodiacal affinity: Uranus.

Keywords: childlike, pure, incorruptible, impulsive, optimistic, spontaneous, adventurous.

take risks that make others fearful for us, but ultimately we are prepared to dive head-first into life itself, oblivious of the dangers that may or may not befall. The Fool, however, does have his bag of provisions with him, indicating he is not entirely foolhardy, and that we should take care to provide not only for our own well-being but also for that of others.

The journeys made by The Fool are ultimately those that take place inside all people, which can happen by making real journeys, having new experiences and undertaking new projects or new relationships. Take advantage of The Fool's inner strength and imagination, but make sure your own 'foolishness' hides a greater wisdom beneath the surface. The Fool seeks the profound truth that lies behind the mask of simple things, and by discovering himself first, discovers the deeper wisdom.

end. He represents the soul that sets out on a voyage of self-discovery that may appear 'foolish' in the eyes of the world. But if he perseveres and attains the wisdom of heaven which lies within, then perhaps he will become the wise one and not those who so blindly ridicule him.

If the whole Tarot were to be condensed into one card it would be The Fool. Here lies the courage, that others take for foolishness, to set off on adventures that deepen not only our material and emotional lives, but also bestow the inner wisdom of a life truly lived. This card indicates profound and bizarre mysteries and experiences that cause us to grow into deeply aware individuals. We may be ridiculed, we may occasionally

1. THE MAGICIAN

The Magician stands tall, straight and confident. He wears a long red robe and is surrounded by white lilies and red roses – the traditional symbols of life and death. Here he is shown with his right hand holding a lighted candle up to Heaven, while his left hand points down to Earth. This symbolizes his ability to bridge the gap between the two, having learned to be a vehicle for divine manifestations. Above his head is the sign of the Holy Spirit (wisdom) which, like an endless cord, forms the lemniscate of infinity, suggesting the endless transmission and transformation of universal energy that moves in a continuous cycle through all things. His silver belt, in the form of a snake swallowing its own tail (the *ouroboros*), signifies eternity, indicating how the lemniscate also operates on the earthly plane, where our own cycles of energy allow us to choose what we make manifest and what we let die.

On the table in front of The Magician are the symbols of the Minor Arcana: the cup, the sword, the wand and the pentacle, which indicate that he is the one who makes things happen in the world. Here the innate energy of the universe is combined with our own creative energy on the ground. The

Zodiacal affinity: Mercury.

Keywords: persuasive, aware, conscious, active, manipulative, powerful, creative.

Magician has power over the elements, power over others, and ultimately power over himself. He is in control, he knows how things work and can analyze them in detail. He takes action and things happen.

Creative energy is a powerful force that lives within us all. The Magician accesses it through his knowledge of the law 'as above, so below'. He marshals his thoughts and feelings towards seeing his dreams as if they were already realities, and having no doubt or fear, they are naturally fulfilled.

45

2. THE HIGH PRIESTESS

The High Priestess replaces action with receptivity, which leads to the uncovering of immense knowledge from deep within herself. She sits, glowing like the Moon, between the two pillars of light and dark (Boaz and Jachim). She embodies intuition, instinct and esoteric knowledge. She does not seek to dissect but relies on synthesis, on the bringing together of opposites. Thus she is light and dark, active and passive, merciful and severe. Like The Magician, she exists between realms and so acts as a conduit, or vessel, holding the wisdom of what is above and below within herself. Note how the Torah lies rolled up in her hands and held over the left side of her chest, as if to say, 'you can read this with your heart but not your eyes'.

She is connected with the Moon and her crown shows it in its three phases, associating her with the unconscious and with the feminine. What is interesting is that she was originally known as the 'Papess' or 'Female Pope', based on the legend of Pope Joan, a woman dressed as a man, who became pope during the Middle Ages, signifying that, although female, she was able secretly to attain the highest position in what is ultimately a male spiritual tradition. This story again shows her falling between polarities, female energy existing

Zodiacal affinity: the Moon.

Keywords: intuitive, secretive, mysterious, wise, contemplative, calm, discreet.

46

deep within male authority. Secrets are an important aspect of this card. The High Priestess gains secret knowledge through relating everything she has learned or studied to the wisdom that already exists within herself. She observes her own being and finds that all lessons fall somewhere between the polarities that exist within herself.

The High Priestess is a visionary. She is the repository of our hidden secrets and intuitive understanding of the Universe. She is the perfect teacher because she uses no tricks or makes us learn by rote. She inspires us to awaken the knowledge we already have existing within ourselves, which lies waiting there, ready to be awakened.

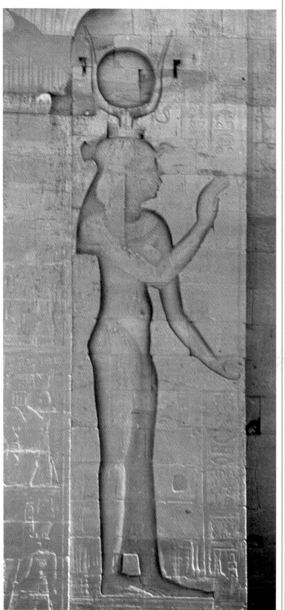

3. THE EMPRESS

The Empress embraces the sensuality and abundance of the Earth because she already possesses them within herself. She sits in a field full of golden wheat, while behind her a waterfall pours into a lake. She wears a pink gown, carries a golden sceptre, and holds a shield bearing the symbol of femininity. This card extols the heart's wisdom and generosity. Unlike the preceding card, The High Priestess, The Empress has no need to keep her femininity and her power a secret. She appears on the Earth, offering her bounty to all. She is aware that her power lies in her femininity; it is both her shield and her active power in the world.

The Empress understands that unconditional love can work magic, but does not use her magic for personal gain. She uses it to the benefit of everything around her and that is why she is Empress of the World. There is enormous power in generosity: The Empress understands that giving everything she has to the world can only lead to greater inner growth. She focuses her energy on growth and so harvests everything within her sphere. She is a maternal symbol whose compassion is devoid of weakness. She will fight to the death to protect her children.

Zodiacal affinity: Venus.

Keywords: sensual, vital, nurturing, generous, compassionate, creative.

The Empress embodies both the sensual lover and the benevolent mother, two aspects which stem from one ultimate quality: the ability to give and receive generously. The Empress listens to those around her. She not only hears what they say but also how they say it. She is aware of the rhythms and cycles of growth or change present within all things, and acts accordingly to bring about the greater good. Consciousness of her own body's sensuality and the workings of her own five senses means she is perfectly attuned to the world. She is rooted to the Earth and nourishes everything within it. Her greatest gifts to mankind are growth, generosity, sensuality and passion.

4. THE EMPEROR

The Emperor is a natural leader, having either been born to the role or having already disposed of anyone standing in his way. He sits on a throne, flanked by two rams' heads, which indicate the astrological sign Aries, associated with power, initiative and dominion. He holds an orb and a sceptre, which bears the *ankh* at its tip, being the Egyptian symbol for life. The Emperor understands that in order to generate productivity the creative energy of the Earth must be domesticated and taught how to work for mankind. As a farmer ploughs a field by harnessing his animals and putting them to work, so The Emperor cultivates the soul by reining in the passions through the creation of inner laws. These are not the divine laws we find exemplified in The Hierophant, but are the fundamental rules by which we learn to live in society.

In the preceding card, The Empress, we see the idea of having a sensual union with the world around us. In this card, The Emperor teaches how at certain times a withdrawal from the state of union is necessary so that order can be created out of chaos. Imposing our will upon ourselves

Zodiacal affinity: Aries.

Keywords: powerful, controlling, patriarchal, authoritative, rigid, stable, inflexible, traditional, organized.

and our surroundings can be necessary, but The Emperor also warns of a desire to dominate and smother those around us. Here we see the image of the angry father, who must be obeyed at all times. Control of the passions is often necessary, but control for the sake of power alone is likely to stifle us and make our lives more difficult. The Emperor wears a very heavy crown, signifying that he has been in control for so long that he has begun to buckle under the weight of his own authority.

With The Emperor comes the drive to create law and order and become our own authority. Here, we channel our intuitive nature into the dualities 'yes' and 'no' and learn how to impose our will on our surroundings to create stability and harmony. But domination comes at a heavy price: it demands that we remove ourselves from intimacy with others and so impose ourselves above or apart from our surroundings. The Emperor knows that this separation is necessary, but that it comes at a heavy price. If he's not careful he may become cold, detached and entirely obsessed with the necessity to control.

The Emperor has managed to stifle the generosity and passion of The Empress archetype within himself. When the two archetypes are balanced, then the soul is both nourished and in control of its passions. When The Emperor archetype predominates, humanity has been sacrificed for the sake of power.

5. THE HIEROPHANT

The role of The Hierophant in religion is to bring the laity into the presence of that which is deemed holy. The word comes from the Greek, being the combination of *ta hiera*, 'the holy', and *phainein*, 'to show', and was the title of priests presiding over the Eleusinian Mysteries. The Hierophant is an interpreter of sacred mysteries and arcane principles. He bestows his blessing and teaches us how to receive divine grace. He sits on a throne, his right hand raised in benediction over the two monks who kneel at his feet. In his left hand is a sceptre resembling a papal cross, which has two smaller crossbars each side of the main crossbar. These echo the three lines in his crown and represent the union of The Empress and The Emperor in their creation of a third person: The Hierophant himself. In him, the generosity of nature (The Empress) combines with the intellectual will of humankind (The Emperor), but this doesn't complete the story. The Hierophant balances these two horizontal or worldly dimensions of being and raises them to a vertical awareness that there is something greater than Heaven or Earth or even self.

The two crossed keys below his feet repeat this lesson, symbolizing the union of two different kinds of knowledge until a third, deeper knowledge

Zodiacal affinity: Taurus.

Keywords: disciplined, conservative, conforming, mature, moral, orthodox, respectful, dogmatic.

In that he represents conformity to both social and moral standards, and is a teacher of great insight and wisdom, The Hierophant knows that every material or self-oriented question has a spiritual counterpart. Paradoxically, however, the spiritual answers to these questions usually come when we stop looking for them. They may not satisfy our immediate desires, but they are guaranteed to open up new dimensions of understanding that will ultimately affect not only our questions but also our whole way of thinking and of experiencing the world.

This complex card points to advice being sought that may fundamentally alter our perspectives. The danger with The Hierophant, however, is that he is not rooted solely in the everyday world, and may become dogmatic and overly self-righteous when his views are challenged. He is more often associated with the outer or religious path rather than the inner and the esoteric, but at his most subtle level neither of these is true.

appears within us and frees us from both of these worlds. This is achieved by grace rather than by our own efforts.

The Hierophant represents organized religion, and seen negatively can forewarn against dogmatism, rigidity and moral superiority. It also indicates a strong sense of morality, or 'right and wrong', and often points to the intervention in our affairs of a 'master' or 'guru' figure. This card is connected with the idea of receiving blessing, which is the blessing that bestows grace itself. Only by relinquishing the notion of 'self' will we find the place within us, that moves us beyond heaven and earth and which is where esotericism and mysticism merge.

6. THE LOVERS

Here a pair of lovers stand together naked, like Adam and Eve in the Garden of Eden. Each has their own tree bearing fruit. Eve's tree traditionally holds the serpent that urges her to separate herself from the divine grace (exemplified in the preceding Hierophant card) and choose between right and wrong for herself, which is where we find the beginnings of doubt. Doubt needs to be experienced so that discrimination can be developed, whereas faith requires no further testing or close examination.

The Lovers are watched over by a fiery angel, who holds his hands, palms upward, towards Heaven. The card symbolizes not only physical love but also life-long platonic friendships and lasting bonds that suggest that another kind of commitment has been made.

Without experiencing human love, with the difficult choices and sacrifices that it involves, how is it possible to approach divine or spiritual love? Falling in love indicates we are ready to abandon aspects of our former lives or former selves. This is because love isn't only a sensual or erotic feeling but also suggests something deeper: that we have grown to love another person's soul.

Zodiacal affinity: Gemini.

Keywords: commitment, temptation, completeness, love, choice, romance, desire, harmony.

lover and experience emotional pain before continuing our current journey without them. But if we embark upon a new life together we are making a journey into the unknown. This is the choice exemplified by The Lovers. Although we may be experiencing doubt we have made our own decisions and are willing to suffer the relative joys and disappointments that the future will inevitably hold.

The Lovers emerge from their Garden of Eden and begin to examine what it is that they desire. They have not totally turned their backs on their previous idyllic lives, for the angel continues to watch over them. But they are now combining trust and faith with their own experiences of the outside world. Choosing love requires the courage to be transformed, which might include compromising aspects of our previous lives for our lover, such as our home, our time and so on, but might also indicate greater choices, such as abandoning previous partners, family and country for our beloved. The Lovers, while listening to the angel, see each other and choose whether or not they will develop this love.

The Lovers card indicates a process of maturation, because ultimately there is a sacrifice of sorts to be made. If we choose the status quo, then we will lose our

7. THE CHARIOT

The Chariot exemplifies the use of will and mastery in order to conquer the doubts and divisions within the self and triumph victoriously in the world. It is interesting that the card is called 'The Chariot' and not 'The Charioteer', for we plainly see a man driving a large golden chariot. He has a glowing star above his head and holds a sword in his right hand. Perhaps the key to this card is that even when we have achieved mastery over our passions, and dispelled the doubts that might prevent us from moving forward, we are wise to retain a humble heart.

The Chariot shows a man seemingly in total control of the forces within, yet a union of opposites is signified. The sphinxes pulling it forward are mythological beings, which traditionally used riddles to reveal mankind's frailty and humanity. Here, they are in opposing colours (like the pillars in the The High Priestess card) and seem to be pulling against one another. If they were not under the strict control of the charioteer they would possibly tear the whole vehicle in half. The charioteer has mastered the sphinxes by understanding their riddle: he

Zodiacal affinity: Cancer.

Keywords: conquest, honour, victory, energy, egocentric, self-confident, conviction, willpower, success, anxiety.

may have phenomenal power but he is still human, and possesses all the frailty to which mankind is heir.

In this card we move on from the doubt and hesitation of the preceding Lovers and forge ahead with total faith in ourselves. The charioteer has been able to pull himself together and show how he can propel himself forward by the power of his will into a rewarding future. His chariot, however, is not totally under his control, for the forces actually propelling it are waiting for him to make a mistake; they will pull him in opposite directions if for one second he lowers his guard.

The star above his ahead indicates that he progresses only because of divine sanction, and he would do well to keep this thought in mind. Without the humility that reminds us we are not the masters of our own fate he is likely to commit the sin of pride. In order to achieve the phenomenal victory that he seeks, he has to remember that without The Chariot, the charioteer has no hope of achieving his goal.

8. STRENGTH

The Strength card shows how the subtle workings of the ego can be controlled. A woman, dressed in white, has gently prised the jaws of a lion apart. She wears a belt of spring flowers that encircles her waist and also the lion's neck. Above her head is the lemniscate, indicating infinity. Whatever the charioteer, shown in the previous card, was hiding from himself and the world for fear it might tear him apart, the woman in this card is tackling it head-on. She has gone right to the source of the raging conflict within, which is desire itself. The lion's pride has not been wounded by her gentle domination, and he is willing to submit to her and accept her garland. This is because she has approached him with gentleness,

Zodiacal affinity: Leo.

Keywords: self-control, patience, compassion, composure, stability, perseverance, moderation.

purity and love. What this action symbolizes is the ease with which the inner beast within us all, which threatens to assault reason and create jealousy, anger or revenge, can be tamed. The lemniscate, seen also in the image of The Magician, indicates the woman understands the universal workings of ebb and flow, and can direct this knowledge towards enhancing her higher self. The Magician, however, is using his understanding of such things to further himself in the material world.

Strength first involves an awareness of the universal knowledge, then self-knowledge, and finally mastery over our base desires. Here, the lion, despite his egotism, is not telling Strength what to do, whom to desire, in which direction to go, it is the other way around. She achieves this not through will or arcane knowledge, but by means of the most fundamental aspect of her nature; she is saying, here I am, without fear, and the lion is only too happy to submit.

59

9. THE HERMIT

The Hermit holds the lamp of the inner wisdom that shines in the darkness, ready to undertake the inner journey by withdrawing from the world. The Hermit symbolizes introspection, analysis and chastity and he is clad in a white robe. He holds a tall staff in his left hand and a lamp in the other, with a light shining brightly from it in the form of a six-pointed star. Interestingly, in this deck, his eyes are closed, indicating that his long, meditative journey has already begun.

A six-pointed star, or hexagram, contains two equal-sided triangles when superimposed on one another, one with its apex pointing up, the other pointing down. The one pointing down indicates the inward journey and is related to the element of water, while that which points up indicates the outward journey and is related to the element of fire. Thus the two triangles represent the alchemical reconciliation of the opposites of fire and water symbolized within the lantern. The two light triangles within the star are metaphors for the two life journeys that will eventually merge into one.

The archetype of the Hermit or the wise old man exists in all world literature. Whether or not this teacher appears on the physical, outer plane,

Zodiacal affinity: Virgo.

Keywords: detachment, discrimination, discretion, withdrawal, introspection, analysis, chastity.

or on the inner plane through dreams and visions, doesn't really matter. He is guided by wisdom itself, uniting all the disparate aspects of self by means of knowledge or gnosis.

The Hermit is withdrawing from the world in order to re-evaluate his life. The card that follows, The Wheel of Fortune, indicates a turning point. Thus, before turning this page in our lives, we must often withdraw and undertake a process of self-examination before emerging to make an effective change. This is the period of quiet introspection that occurs before the violent upheaval of flux begins.

10. THE WHEEL OF FORTUNE

The wheel spins, and blind Fortuna suddenly has us within her grasp. This card shows the wheel placed inside a tomb, with Anubis, the Egyptian jackal-headed god on the left, and a snake on the right, these being symbols of death and transformation. Whatever way the wheel turns there is a death of sorts awaiting us. This is not fatal, but points to a shift in consciousness that is so deeply buried that we may not even be aware of it until something in our lives reflects, in strange, unaccountable ways, that a change has occurred within. This card marks a turning point in our lives, and it is no accident that it appears directly in the centre of the Tarot (see The Hermit). It is only vanity that makes us assume we can control everything in our lives. When the Wheel of Fortune turns we have to accept that dynamic spiritual forces are working within us to move us along our path, the only way forward being to surrender to them. Whatever our fate we must remember that the 'self' that moves through these changes is ultimately irrelevant and powerless to change what has been ordained.

Much as we may think we can master our fate through introspection and self-knowledge, the

Zodiacal affinity: Jupiter.

Keywords: luck, inevitability, timing, destiny, turning point, synchronicity, unpredictability.

Wheel of Fortune demonstrates how all our careful work and planning can suddenly be rendered useless. Once the soul or inner consciousness is ready to open itself to a new truth nothing will stay unchanged.

The Wheel of Fortune, in its four corners, shows the symbols of the four fixed astrological signs, Taurus, Leo, Scorpio and Aquarius, which have no power to prevent the wheel from turning and throwing our carefully-laid plans up in the air. Around the wheel itself are some letters, written in gold, which, if read clockwise, spell out 'Tora', which is the Judaic book of law and wisdom. If we read the letters anti-clockwise the word 'Taro' is spelled out, which is the esoteric wisdom we are exploring here. Interspersed between the letters are smaller ones spelling out the ancient and

inscrutable name of God, Yahweh (I-H-V-H). Thus, whether we follow the outer journey, Tora, or the inner journey, Taro, we will find that the unity of all things runs through both, brought together through the name of God.

Whenever the Wheel of Fortune turns or changes direction, either the inner journey or the outer journey is thrown into chaos, shifting our consciousness and adding confusion. This is because whatever path we are following ultimately leads to the same goal. Once we have learned that we can be sure of nothing, then we have learned the lesson being taught. We then learn to go with the flow, remaining attached to nothing, whether they be outward possessions or spiritual insights we thought we understood.

11. JUSTICE

Justice is traditionally the eighth card and Strength the 11th, but their position was switched in the influential Rider-Waite deck to make them better fit the astrological correspondences adopted by the Hermetic Order of the Golden Dawn. Justice is shown as a woman sitting on a throne. In one hand she holds the gleaming sword of accountability, and in the other a pair of scales (Libra) signifying the balanced view. Images of Justice are usually blindfolded, signifying impartiality, but in this deck Justice has her eyes wide open, having come to understand why she is here. The card indicates that it is now time to take responsibility for events that we have set in motion.

In a sense, we have moved on from the last card, The Wheel of Fortune, which shows how little control we have over our lives. Here Justice asks us to acknowledge and understand how our past thoughts, words and deeds have come to create the present issues uppermost in our lives. The double-edged sword indicates that whatever way we 'cut' or choose, each decision has its consequences, the way we made these important choices being dependent on the way our personal histories have been allowed to shape our

Zodiacal affinity: Libra.

Keywords: harmony, equality, balance, equilibrium, fairness, responsibility, interaction, communication.

characters. When Justice prevails, the idea of fate or destiny is prevalent, which does not mean we have no choice because it had already been made for us. In fact, it means the reverse. If we find that the same issues keep recurring in our lives, it's probably because we have refused to admit to

ourselves, on a deeper level, how little we have done to mend our ways.

Here, our fate is in our own two hands, our past actions having set a course of events in motion. We need to take responsibility for our lives and discover how we have got to this point, then, with this self-knowledge firmly in our minds, we can learn to commit to decisions that are rooted in the present, rather than repeating the same old mistakes of the past. Justice has no time for excuses and denials. By drawing a line, dividing the past from the present, we can decide where it is that we want to go and what it is that we need to leave behind.

12. THE HANGED MAN

The Hanged Man understands the value of sacrifice. The gallows from which he is suspended forms a Tau cross, and his head appears to be veiled in cloud. It should also be noted that the tree of sacrifice is in fact living wood, in that it is bearing leaves. The man hangs upside-down from the tree, his left leg bent behind his right. If he were to be reversed to an upright position we would see that his legs form the number 4. There is no suggestion of pain and he seems to be almost entranced, for he has willingly sacrificed something in order to gain greater wisdom. Nowhere is this image more poignant than the one that exists in Norse mythology, where Odin, the king of the gods, is hung from the Tree of Knowledge in order to claim the wisdom of true kingship.

The 4, in numerology, refers to attributes of the Earth. It represents stability and the four directions, north, south, east, west. An inverted 4 suggests the opposite element of water, which symbolizes the realms of the unconscious and the emotional. Another aspect of this inversion, however, is that it points not to Earth but to Heaven.

Zodiacal affinity: Neptune.

Keywords: transition, paradox, limbo, transition, boredom, progress, adaptation, rebirth.

This card shows how we can reverse our position, our understanding or perspective of something which can result in greater spiritual knowledge. So far, we have run our lives according to a set of beliefs and expectations of ourselves and the world around us. Now, we sacrifice this comfortable position in order to see things from a new angle, and are ready to reach a level of independence. Whatever way we go, gravity will always turn us back the right way. We are creatures of the Earth and we can't forget it, but The Hanged Man reminds us that if we are prepared to

engage willingly in a profound sacrifice we will set in motion the process of gnosis within ourselves. This will render what was earthly spiritual, and what was spiritual earthly. By making a willing sacrifice, we show that we are ready to move on with our lives, having learned the sometimes difficult lesson of detachment in order to attain something altogether greater and far more profound.

13. DEATH

Death sits on a throne of bones. Behind him are two jagged towers between which the sun casts a strong but hazy glow. Two figures, a man and a woman, approach Death with open hands, forced, in the cold light of day, to drop the masks they have been wearing all their lives and face the reality that everything in life eventually comes to a natural end, when they must inevitably face the simple truth of who they really are.

Apart from physical death, this card symbolizes the death of the persona, which is the enhanced image of ourselves that we present to others, heralding the moment when the internal and external forces that surround us cause us to drop the mask beneath which we have remained hidden for most of our lives. The word 'persona' literally means a mask, indicating a character played by an actor. In other words, it is the image of ourselves which may be far from true that we have chosen to present, and that we believe makes it easier for us to operate in the world. But if we come to believe in this persona, forgetting that there is a real person behind the mask, then we are deceiving not only the world but also ourselves. It is then likely that our energy will become

Zodiacal affinity: Scorpio.

Keywords: change, beginnings, endings, transformation, relinquishment, acceptance.

dangerously undermined by the effort needed to cultivate and maintain this spurious self-image.

In life the Death card indicates that it is time for us to face reality, that will enable us to drop the mask and make irrevocable changes that will reveal who we really are, both to ourselves and others. This is a powerful and painful process. Whereas The Hanged Man willingly sacrifices himself in order to understand this truth, the Death card suggests that the opportunity for total change has arrived and that there is little we can do but rise to the challenge. The fact that certain aspects of our lives must end before transformation can be effected is feared only before we take this daunting step, never afterwards, even though it requires us to undergo

not one but several little deaths before we can emerge into the light of truth with a greatly expanded understanding of what it means to be mortal. In the natural world, the death of winter paves the way for the emergence of spring; in other words, Death promises that before long everything will be entirely different.

14. TEMPERANCE

Temperance unites the polarities of the self, effecting a more profound integration. The card shows an angel with wings the colour of terra cotta. His gown is white, the breast of which bears a square in which a golden triangle is contained, its apex pointing up. He is standing with one foot in a stream, the other on land, and is pouring water from a golden cup into another holding wine, so diluting it. In the distance, between two mountains, the golden crown of the sun sheds its light on the world. The Temperance card symbolizes the blending or synthesis of opposites to achieve moderation and balance. It indicates that we have now obliterated false aspects of self and have emerged as one, well-integrated person. We no longer place such immovable boundaries between the spiritual and the material within us.

The golden triangle symbolizes Heaven harmoniously resting within the square that represents Earth. In this deck, the colour of the angel's wings also suggests integration between the material and spiritual worlds. It is important that the image of the triangle inside the square appears over the angel's heart, in that the heart performs the physical function of circulating the blood around

Zodiacal affinity: Sagittarius.

Keywords: moderation, compromise, virtue, self-control, harmony, understanding, transcendence, synthesis.

the body. On a spiritual level, the energetic heart-centre could be said to purify our spiritual energies, causing them to flow more effectively within us. The sun, which appeared so cold but intense in the preceding card, Death, has been transformed into a crown, symbolizing that what we once refused to face in the cold light of day has now become our greatest strength.

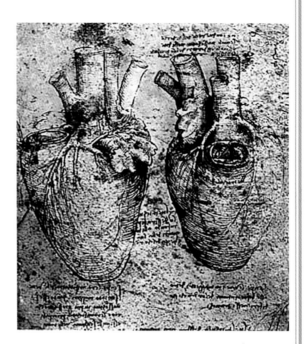

These transformations have been effected through the angelic principle of pure love that has been allowed to enter our stream of consciousness to effect changes to the energies and desires within us. This creates a feeling of well-being and a sense that things are 'as they should be'. Our energies are now working for us, rather than being dissipated by false notions of self.

This card indicates the virtues of patience and harmony. We are learning to move beyond the mode of 'either/or' and understand the wisdom of 'both', togetherness and compatibility being aspects of this card, as well as a high level of creativity. Our ideas can now be allowed to flow effortlessly, because they are no longer being obstructed by internal boundaries and oppositions.

15. THE DEVIL

The Devil indicates the self-enslavement which prevents us from growing. It is the obsessional behaviour that we know is harmful but from which we cannot escape. But it can represent another kind of rigid mindset, indicating an over-restrained, doggedly pragmatic person, who is unable to let their hair down from time to time. The card shows a man and a woman chained to a platform or altar on which the Devil stands. His right hand is raised, fingers open, and his left, holding a flaming torch, points downward. An inverted pentacle, the symbol of power, is imposed on his forehead. The man and woman, each with long tails winding around their bodies, stand face-to-face, gazing at one another. The position of The Devil and his arms reminds us of The Magician card, but there is a crucial difference. Whereas The Magician's raised arm points one finger to the sky to indicate a knowledge of the forces of Heaven, The Devil's open hand denotes he believes only in his own power, the power of his five senses, and that there is nothing beyond. Thus The Devil is a slave to earthly delights and it is his materialism and stagnation that chains us to him.

If our drives and desires are the centre of our universe, leaving space for little else, then it is not

Zodiacal affinity: Capricorn.

Keywords: materialism, temptation, bondage, greed, addiction, negativity, hedonism, passion, egotism.

surprising that they should become obsessions. The preceding card, Temperance, shows an integrated person living according to the angelic principles of patience and harmony. The Devil is the absolute obverse, indicating a person whose consciousness is centred around their own desires. At this point it is important to note that a second aspect of the preceding card, Temperance, is its sense of hope, and accordingly, a second aspect of The Devil is fear – fear of our desires, fear of oppression, fear of our shadow nature. What we come to learn is that hope and fear are two aspects of our nature that ultimately prevent us from living in the world, in that both hope and fear are fixed

our inner demon is to release ourselves from its chains, and will enable us to experience true freedom at last.

not on what is, but on what might be. This detracts from what we have in our lives right now, and so makes it difficult to remain centred or effect change.

Our desires are only to be feared when they are focused on a single object, be it obsession with a person, status or anything that reduces us to the position of a slave. Learning to face

16. THE TOWER

The Tower indicates a total collapse of everything we have built up around us, forcing us to confront our illusions. The card shows a tall, grey tower being struck by lightning, from which a king and a queen are falling. The sky is grey and filled with storm clouds. On one level, The Tower presages the loss of everything we hold dear, which, on the material level, can mean our relationships, our livelihoods, our home and so on. One of the key meanings of this card, however, is that breakdown or break-up often leads to breakthrough.

This card depicts a tower that raises its inhabitants above the earth, rather as the biblical Tower of Babel was built to unite people and bring them close to God. It was destroyed because its true purpose was forgotten, obliterated because of the overweening pride of its architects. Although we are powerful to a degree, we must never forget we are still mortal.

The Tower represents a catastrophic blow to the ego. In the preceding card, The Devil, we are the slaves of our desires through obsession and an inability to see anything beyond satisfying them. The Tower has been blown apart because we no longer know who we are and what is our true

Zodiacal affinity: Mars.

Keywords: revelation, unexpected events, chaos, sudden change, hard times, crisis, disruption, realizing the truth.

74

we cannot know who we are or where we are going until we remember, on the deepest level, whence we came. In the card, the domesticated dog stares at the wild one, the latter having been part of the former's evolutionary process, so that neither can exist without knowledge of the other. In the same way, we are urged to enter the deep, forgotten parts of our unconscious where uncomfortable aspects of ourselves remain hidden out of sight even to ourselves.

In this deck, the creature in the pool is a fantastical monster, whereas in other decks it is a crayfish or a crab. But the thing that they have in common is that they are scaly and impenetrable. These represent the monstrous fears that lie dormant in the unconscious mind, and is because the persona we show to the world

is often so much at odds with our everyday selves as to become frightening. Like the dog and the wolf in the picture, we have to embrace and reconcile that which exists both within and out. The process of examining these deep and monstrous wounds can be difficult and must be approached with care, but we will never be able to aspire to the heights without first plumbing these unfathomable depths. The longer our darker selves remain hidden, the more likely they are to erupt when we least expect it. By breaking the hypnotic power The Moon exerts on us we will find that we are ready to move on to the next card, The Sun. Learning the lesson of The Moon, we bring the shadowy aspects of ourselves out into the true light, thus breaking the debilitating aspects of their power and embracing our own evolution.

19. THE SUN

The Sun teaches us to enjoy being human and thus connects us with the intrinsic joy present in everything around us. In this card the Sun is so bright as to be all-pervasive, as if everything around it is being drawn in and absorbed by its rays. Its heat is nourishing, and permeates every living thing. The process of photosynthesis is a simple reality of science, but this light is the light of revelation, that all things are brought uniquely alive through its beneficence. Once we have absorbed this simple truth, the joyful experience of an ecstatic outpouring will follow, teaching us the lesson of the 19th card of the Major Arcana.

Two naked children, one on a horse, which is white and docile, and one on the ground, are holding a red cloth between them. They are seeing the world around them with fresh, exploratory eyes. There is no competition, conflict or dissimulation between them, for they have learned the lesson, 'as above, so below'. Both are sharing the same feelings of joy, regardless of whether they are on the horse or on the ground. Here, co-operation is the key. As all living things rely on the sun, without which they would soon die, so The Sun reveals our interdependence on one another, which is outwardly expressed by showing

Zodiacal affinity: the Sun.

Keywords: joy, positive energy, happiness, sharing, creativity, growth, optimism, enthusiasm, radiance.

compassion, loving kindness and transmitting joy from one heart to another. But on a deeper and more fundamental level it underlies the unity of all living things.

The children in the card still have their perfect innocence totally intact, and they will remain happy and in harmony until it is inevitably lost. But we can still feel something of the joy and wonder of those far-off days by surrendering ourselves to the stream of renewal and revelation that teaches us to live each moment as fully as possible, looking at the world

through child-like eyes. Here we are unhampered by the unresolved issues of the preceding card, The Moon. We have learned not to repeat our mistakes by savouring each new moment as it comes. Joy, gratitude and love: what better virtues are there than these three.

20. JUDGEMENT

As the Judgement card symbolizes resurrection, or God's promise of eternal life after death, so too can it herald the return of individuals from the past. It may also represent a preoccupation with the past, while at the same time calling forth new beginnings after ridding ourselves of the past. The picture shows an angel, crowned with the Sun, blowing a golden trumpet from which a banner bearing a red cross hangs. Three figures stand naked before it, a mother, father and child, their backs turned towards us.

This is a card of renewal and restoration, which does not return the status quo but elevates all we have thought, done and said to a new, higher plane. Notice how the angel is crowned with the sun; The Sun card referred to a renewal of joy through unity or connectedness. Judgement takes this rush of joy and directs it towards altruism, prompting compassion and generosity. This is why the mother, father and child appear, in that they are the symbols of the divine lying within the human family.

Here the idea of return is explored, in that it indicates retrieving something that has been lost. Whatever we've lost is often returned to us, but by now we are so different that we value it in a new

Zodiacal affinity: Pluto.

Keywords: liberation, transformation, judgement, rebirth, release from the past.

and higher way. Returning what was lost to others is also indicated, the most profound form of which is the rekindling of joy, lightness and trust in another person.

As mentioned previously, Judgement is usually a preliminary to resurrection, the first historical accounts of which were developed within a Zoroastrian context. This cosmology suggests that a Saviour would restore the world from all the perils of the angry or evil spirits according to God's wish, the Saviour actively participating in the gift of renewal that he or she has received. In the same way, we are asked to examine our past actions and make internal recompense before ascending to a higher level of awareness.

We have worked through the stages of the Major Arcana with courage, generosity and creativity and all our hard work is now rewarded. But the act of receiving is not passive, especially here, where we actively infuse everything around us with renewed generosity because we have been able to banish self-interest and cultivate a lasting unselfishness of spirit. On a spiritual level, all we touch now turns to gold, in that we have become a simile for gold itself.

21. THE WORLD

The World represents an ending to a cycle of life, a pause before the next cycle beginning with The Fool recommences. The figure on the card dances suspended between the heavens and the earth, symbolizing completeness. The figure is surrounded by a wreath, representing water, and the four corners of the card echo what is written in the Book of Revelation, 4:7, 'And the first beast was like a lion, and the second beast like a calf, and the third beast had a face as a man, and the fourth beast was like a flying eagle.' Together, they make up the five elements, water, fire, earth, spirit and air. We glimpse, for a moment, the dancer as the centre of the universe, the eternal spirit or the ultimate truth. The World, or The Universe, as it is sometimes called, is the card of art, which in this context can refer to human artistic endeavour but also indicates the artistry of creation, in that all things manifest and non-manifest are expressions of divine, creative love.

The World joins with the first arcanum, The Fool, to reveal the continuous cycle of life, death and rebirth. The Fool (symbolizing the human soul in search of enlightenment) recommences his journey, but The World returns him to the same position but with ultimate freedom and the

Zodiacal affinity: Saturn.

Keywords: fulfilment, accomplishment, success, integration, involvement, freedom.

knowledge that everything he does and everywhere he goes is a game being played for the sake of 'being' alone. He is becoming less attached to earthly things, consequently his search for ultimate wisdom will be that much easier.

This card returns us to the physical plane having accomplished profound creative successes, precisely because we are no longer chasing illusory needs or personal desires. We relax our grip on the demands of the ego and so become a polished mirror through which universal forces can play themselves out. The five elements of the worldly plane remind us that the workings of the earth and that of the universal stream of consciousness have entirely merged. We now understand the paradox that our purpose has no purpose, and that no purpose is without essential meaning. Beauty, art, journeys and successes, these are all ours because we have removed the fundamental obstacle that lies between them and us: the notion of 'I'.

CHAPTER THREE

THE MINOR ARCANA

The Minor Arcana teach the lessons of everyday life. They do not refer to profound shifts of consciousness, as do the Major Arcana, but point to the workings of the world around us. For this reason, they are used for divination or to seek knowledge of the future.

When working with the Minor Arcana, it is important to develop your own relationship with the cards. Before you start, try laying the cards out in groups organized according to their suits. What suit attracts you the most? Which do you find troubling? Which corresponds most closely to your journey? With which one do you find it difficult to connect? As you learn more about the cards you will find that the answers you gave to these first questions reveal a lot about the way you personally handle the world around you. Once you begin to understand yourself, you will find that

you will be better able to identify what is going on in the lives of other people.

The Minor Arcana are often linked with the ancient Judaic mystical tradition, known as the Kabbala, that used esoteric ciphers to interpret the Bible, but it is not necessary to have a deep knowledge of this in order to read the Tarot. What is important is the use of the Kabbala's Tree of Life, bearing spheres (*sefirot*) interconnected by pathways, to assist in interpreting the minor cards.

In this, the numbers 1 to 10 are arranged in the form of a 'tree' (see opposite) that symbolizes how the Universe first came into being.

On taking your first look at the Minor Arcana, look at the key words appropriate to each number. At first glance they seem to make little sense, but when the pathways linking them are explored, interesting ideas will begin to emerge. This will prove to be

KEY TO THE TREE OF LIFE

1-Keter	*Crown (Ace)*
2-Chochma	*Wisdom*
3-Binah	*Understanding*
4-Chesed	*Mercy*
5-Gevurah	*Severity*
6-Tiferet	*Beauty*
7- Netzach	*Victory*
8-Hod	*Glory*
9-Yesod	*Foundation*
10-Malchut	*Kingdom*

a lengthy process, so try not to let yourself become disheartened. Remember that you are embarking on your own journey, and that your conclusions will be personal to you, making your approach to reading the cards unique and special.

Now the 16 Court cards must be mentioned, the King, Queen, Knight and Page of each respective suit,

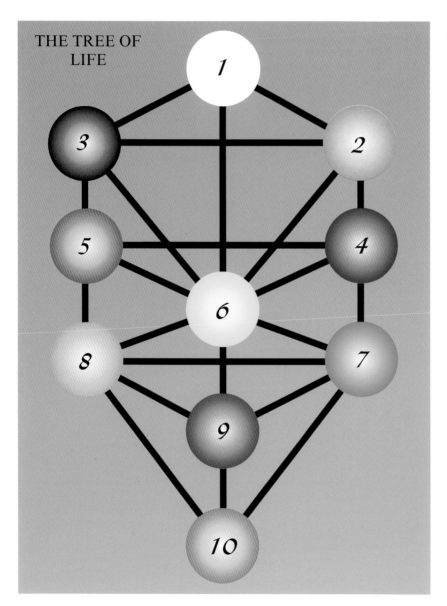

THE TREE OF
LIFE

ABOVE: *Examples of Court cards*

LEFT: *The Kabbalistic Tree of Life is useful for interpreting the Minor Arcana, although it does not give up its secrets easily.*

know, basing your choice on how much they remind you of them. We do this because although the Court cards do not always represent people in a reading, they sometimes do. When a Court card does not represent an actual person, but shows a situation or circumstance, take all the characteristics of that person and apply it to the situation described. If you were to equate the Queen of Wands, for example, with a fiery, passionate woman, to whom you would disclose your ideas but not your emotions, then the person whose card

before we begin the task of interpretation. Lay them out separately and look at each one in turn. Notice the colours used, the background to the main figures, and where the centre of energy seems to lie in each card. Which one of these cards is you? Which one seems to have an affinity with your best friend, or a member of your family? Then go on to ascribe each of the other cards to people you

Of the Court cards in today's playing cards, the Knight has disappeared, leaving only the King, Queen and Page (Knave or Jack), see above, of the esoteric Tarot.

it is may be engaged in an exciting creative project that needs support and direction if it is going to work.

It is interesting to note that when the *Tarot*, *Tarocchi* or *Tarock* became widespread in Medieval Europe it was used in different trick-taking games and in cartomancy (fortune-telling). The 78-card deck then contained 22 cards (known in divination as the Major Arcana) which functioned as a permanent suit of trumps, together with 56 cards (in divination the Minor Arcana) of four suits (either the Anglo-French hearts, diamonds, spades and clubs or the original Latin suits of cups, pentacles, swords, wands), numbered one through ten, plus four Court cards – a Page (Jack), a Knight, a Queen, and a King, of which the Knights were later omitted. Thus we see the Minor Arcana as the basis of our modern pack of playing cards, The Fool being the only card of the Major Arcana to have survived as the 'wild card' or joker.

There is a certain poetry in this, in that life itself can be seen as a game to be played, and that even though the stakes may be high, there is an ultimate prize to be won.

The Suit of Cups is that which is most directly related to the emotions and to the element water. Water is passive, taking its shape from that of its container, before it decides (in human terms) whether it likes where it is or not. Cups is the suit of love and feeling. It shows how we are affected by our feelings and the bearing they have on the situations in which we are involved. Emotions have a deep, intuitive power, often dictating our responses to the people and situations around us. When we react emotionally and intuitively, rather than intellectually and pragmatically, the results are often more effective as a result.

Cups also reveal whether the energy of emotion is blocked or flowing freely in a situation. They won't always tell us what emotion we are feeling, which is up to us to work out, but they will tell us how our our current emotions are affecting our lives. This suit works on one of the deepest levels of our consciousness, casting light on the feelings that are lying beneath the surface of our thoughts and desires. It is a suit indicating effect: when we realize where our vulnerabilities and strengths have led us, then we can decide what to do about the situation. But remember that we may not get very far without having experienced the full gamut of human emotions.

ACE OF CUPS

Here, a strong right hand emerges from a cloud, offering a golden cup. The cup overflows with water or wine that falls in five streams into a pool or lake below, where nine lotus flowers float on its surface. Hovering above the cup is a white dove bearing a Eucharistic wafer in its beak. Here the cup is literally overflowing, signifying that a whole new capacity for life is being opened up within us. The water from the single cup falls in five separate streams, symbolizing the five human senses: touch, taste, smell, sight and hearing, the water having come from one single source – joy.

Thus the means by which we sample our world have suddenly become heightened and rejuvenated. This may be because we have a

Keywords: love, deep emotions, desire for intimacy, romance, receptivity, self-expression, new relationships, expansiveness, well-being.

new love in our life, or are experiencing something that is exciting and expanding our consciousness. The presence of the dove indicates that the sensation may be something of a blessing, a gift we have done nothing at all to deserve; we can clear the way, allowing such feelings to flow in, but it is essentially grace or fortune that brings them vividly to life. Now is the time to savour this heady feeling of expansiveness and well-being before directing it towards action.

When the Ace of Cups is drawn, the indication is that a period of new, joyful awakening is about to begin, and the recipient of the card will be feeling the emotional bounty that is waiting for them beyond the horizon. So enjoy the feeling, and don't forget to share some of the joy you have so undeservedly received.

TWO OF CUPS

This card is so powerful that it is almost the equivalent of The Lovers of the Major Arcana. It shows a man and a woman standing together alone on a wide plain. They stare, totally absorbed, into each other's eyes. Above their heads is a golden caduceus, or herald's wand, bearing a lion's head; this suggests there may be danger in the forthcoming transaction. Both partners are equal, symbolized by the fact that they both hold cups. The woman holds her golden cup in her left hand and the man's hand in her right. The man holds her right hand in his left and his golden cup in his right. The two cups touch, completing a circuit enabling the exchange of sexual energy to flow continuously between the two.

There is nothing here to be lost, no hidden agenda or ulterior motive. The two are there out of love alone, not because one is more powerful, richer or stronger than the other. This is a relationship that has no element of competition in it. The healing symbol above their heads reflects this natural flow of healthy, balanced energies.

The message of this card is balance, and the relationship, at this stage, seems to be harmonious. The danger here is that romantic liaisons can become so intense as to become totally exclusive, turning into the kind of infatuation that can be wonderful for a time but which will eventually burn

Keywords: balance, interconnectedness, partnership, intimacy, attraction, infatuation, obsession.

itself out. Infatuation leading to obsession is destined to lead to disappointment unless there is something deeper in the relationship that will endure as passion inevitably fades.

The Two of Cups may also indicate the union of any two entities or concepts, including businesses, groups of people, ideas or talents. Its message, besides the one of keeping a sense of proportion, is to look for one-to-one connections in your life. In established relationships, this is not the time to separate or break apart, but is one where co-operation is indicated. If there is conflict, forgive and allow yourself to be forgiven.

If you are struggling with two choices or tendencies within yourself, seek to reconcile them, while not forgetting the many influences flowing in from outside. The next cards to be drawn will reveal what these influences are.

CUPS

THREE OF CUPS

The card shows three women dancing in a circle in a field filled with Earth's bounty. There are a few clouds in the sky but the overall impression is of pleasant and temperate weather. There is no element of competition here, and the women are dancing together harmoniously without encroaching on one another's space. Each has different-coloured hair and they are also wearing

Keywords: exuberance, friendship, co-operation, celebration, trust, gregariousness, harmony.

be the useless tendency to 'cry over spilt milk'. It also indicates failure to see the good in a given situation and a deep pessimism with regards to the future. We should realize that support outside of ourselves is there for the taking, and that once we have come through the feelings of regret, abandonment, guilt, denial, or whatever other negative emotions are besetting us now, we will re-emerge a different and a stronger person than we were before.

SIX OF CUPS

The card shows two children in a walled garden, the window of their house behind them. The girl stands, waiting to receive the cup the seated boy is offering her. The other cups in the garden are filled with white blooms and the garden is green and fertile. This is a lovely image of childhood and something of a past memory. There's nothing complicated in the picture and it reminds us of the innocence, simplicity and joy that we have come to associate with that time. Not that every childhood is perfect, and it is futile to indulge in feelings of nostalgia for our lost youth. We may also be regretting the sense of playfulness that we have lost as we have matured. The Six of Cups is in fact urging us forward, telling us to forget the past and learn to live more fully in the present.

Although elements of our present lives may not be as perfect as we had hoped, rather than look back we should perhaps use our memories of happier times as a pointer to the future, enabling us to recapture all the old trust, love and laughter now seemingly absent from our lives. It is no surprise that this card should follow on from the lessons of grief and loss taught by the Five of Cups, but the Six of Cups is urging us to rejoice in each new situation as though we were experiencing it for the very first time.

Keywords: childhood, innocence, nostalgia, irresponsibility, playfulness, naivety, reinvigoration.

When the Six of Cups appears in a reading the implication is that whatever you give generously to others will be returned to you with more besides. The card does not promise there will never be a sense of longing in your heart again, but it does mean that a new chapter in your life is about to begin. Although the Six of Cups is associated with childhood, nostalgia or simply the past, it also points to new feelings of revitalization. Attitudes to life, now that they have become more realistic and more hopeful, suddenly make fulfilment an achievable goal. If there is an element of unfinished business lurking in your past, now is the time to deal with it and banish it from your mind.

SEVEN OF CUPS

Here, the silhouetted shape of a man stands naked before seven golden cups. Each one holds something different: a castle, a wreath, jewels, a dragon, a marble head, a snake. In the topmost cup is a shrouded figure which is a perfect image of the silhouetted man. This is the card of wishful thinking and building castles in the air. All our dreams are here, but what do we desire? This is a card that signifies delusion and the building of false hopes, possibly dreaming of a win on the lottery rather that working towards improving our lives for ourselves.

We are all guilty of day-dreaming, but it is when we allow these thoughts to dominate our lives that we lose track of reality. Sometimes, however, these can turn to dark, sad or negative thoughts, like the little voices that tells us we're not good enough. We can end up repeating this pattern of negativity that impacts on our lives, which is when we should recognize how we may have created these feelings by neglecting to find the positivity that also lies within.

The meanings of the symbols in the Seven of Cups are up for debate and they are probably telling us to find our own answers. The most striking image is that in the uppermost cup. Here, crowned by the sun, is the veiled reflection of our higher or authentic selves. We may have many

Keywords: self-indulgence, wishful thinking, laziness, given to fantasizing, unfeasible expectations, being spoiled for choice.

desires and dreams that we wish to realize, but the greatest of all of these is to manifest our truer, higher nature. We may have to experience all the joys and disappointments of realizing, failing and then recreating our wishes before we come to an understanding of what we actually want. When we reach the place of true understanding all our old dreams may begin to seem different from the time when we were less in tune with ourselves. The journey through our desires, whether we achieve them or not, and knowing how we deal with the success of failure of them, is likely to unlock hidden aspects of ourselves that will lead us to true success.

The person drawing this card possibly has difficulty fulfilling their dreams. Having a dream may be a good, positive way of imagining how they may manifest their desires, but by the same token may be producing nothing but empty fantasies. In either case, they are being asked to examine their desires and their current choices.

It is easier to make up our minds when we're not in the grip of desire for a person, status or object, but we can also take the opportunity to learn a lot about ourselves from the objects of our desire. What do our dreams or nightmares tell us about the place we have arrived at in our lives?

109

EIGHT OF CUPS

The Eight of Cups shows a cloaked figure walking away from a path on which there are eight golden cups. He has rejected them, and under cover of darkness walks towards the hills guided by a full moon and a myriad of stars. This card usually carries the meaning of disillusionment and abandonment of things which have failed to be emotionally fulfilling. It also suggests that circumstances have led us to a place where what we have felt safe and contented with up till now is no longer sufficient. So we are leaving our security behind and are launching ourselves into the unknown future that lies ahead. The Seven of Cups signifies a man overwhelmed by choices, this one shows them being resolved.

The way forward may be dark, but we find that we are being guided by the moon, the symbol of dreams, emotions and mysteries, and the bright stars that are full of fresh hope. This is a beautiful night to be leaving. We may have become attached to what we are leaving behind and may even be feeling sorrowful, but we are confident and clear that we are exchanging the limitations of one life for the possibilities of another.

We have painfully come to realize that unfeasible desires prevent any action or any real growth within. Here, we let go of what is

Keywords: change of direction, moving on to better things, self-discovery, turning over a new page, leaving the past behind.

indicates we are entering into or have already achieved a state of grounded, loving happiness. We appear to have a peaceful home, its serenity coming from a family that is pulling together and which is counting its blessings. Alternatively, the card may signify that an end to hostility is possible. If there is fighting around you, it will cease, and if you are at war with yourself, you will find peace. You have learned to give selflessly without needing to be recompensed, appreciatiated or praised. Harmony now reigns, because, unlike the Nine of Cups, everyone's opinion is respected, and it is not the will of a single person that is being imposed on the others.

PAGE OF CUPS

The Page, dressed in rich and beautiful clothes, is standing by a river. One hand rests on his hip, the other holds a golden cup, out of which a fish has magically appeared just as he was about to drink. This indicates that we never know when the creative impulse may present itself. Therefore the card signifies the beginning of creativity or the start of a new project or creative venture. It may also herald the beginning of a new relationship or putting a new perspective on a difficult situation.

The fish, in early Christian symbology, represents Christ, and His disciples were fishermen or fishers of souls, while in other mythologies it often represents the unconscious, the spirit, or the life force within us all. The card heralds the surprising and perplexing arrival of creative thoughts, that come to us unbidden from deep within our unconscious selves. The card can therefore signify that there is a creative energy trying to burst forth, and that your inner self is trying to speak to you, possibly through your dreams or through synchronistic encounters with significant people. The card is also that of the artist or the lover, who ensnares others, drawing them into the fabulous world of his own creation. He is a charismatic person, fond of collecting muses and admirers, or he may himself be the protegé of an older, wiser individual.

Keywords: gifted, artistic, creative, new relationships, charismatic, imaginative lover.

116

CUPS

KNIGHT OF CUPS

The Knight of Cups sits on a white horse which is moving at a slow pace through water. He is the archetypal 'knight in shining armour'. Here the fish symbol is also present as before, used to decorate his armour. Where the Page of Cups stares bemusedly at the fish that has appeared in his cup, the knight goes forward on a romantic or creative quest, but slowly and with caution, approaching the matter seriously and with a strong sense of what is correct. What we see is singlemindedness; he knows what he wants and he intends to get it. Although it may take some time, he prefers to stick to his principles rather than indulge in compromise. But what is our hero's quest? The Knight of Cups is so idealistic, his head so filled with notions of courtly love, that it isn't too much to imagine that he's on his way to rescue some long-forgotten damsel in distress. The card shows a person who would prefer to be seen as a 'saviour' rather than a 'hero' or 'warrior', pointing to a certain nobility of spirit. But he is also easily bored and in constant need of stimulation, while at the same time being artistic and refined. He is amiable and intelligent, but also a dreamer who can easily get carried away. He may be such a gentleman that it takes him longer to achieve his goal than if he

Keywords: singlemindedness, idealism, romantic, imaginative lover, artistic, refined, highly-principled, day-dreamer.

simply got on with the matter in hand without further ado.

The Knight of Cups signifies someone who is highly idealistic but who is unwilling to sacrifice his principles, which may lead to his missing the boat. The danger here is that such people always require a a cause to champion or someone indebted to them, and if they refuse to play his game he is likely to move swiftly on to engage in his next important crusade.

119

QUEEN OF CUPS

Here the queen sits on a golden throne set on a small islet or peninsula that juts out above the sea. She is dressed entirely in blue, which is the colour most associated with healing and communication. In other Tarot decks, she is the only character bearing a closed cup, signifying that she is a deeply wise person. But her wisdom is such that she only reveals what she believes to be necessary at the time. The Queen of Cups draws upon her own intuitions and creative understanding to

Keywords: wisdom, virtue, creativeness, intuition, empathy, compassion, unconditional love, patience, understanding.

make things work. She knows when to offer advice and when to resist. She is a model of loving virtue, one who is purer of heart than most, and who is a loving mother and a loyal friend.

Drawing the Queen of Cups signifies a wise and caring person, whom others see as a healing presence in their lives. But the inverted card may warn of a false friend, motivated by jealousy and vanity that makes them two-faced and manipulative. Such people are often secretive when it comes to their own affairs, but being charming and persuasive they can be extremely seductive. Sometimes we can benefit from their advice, but make sure first that no ulterior motives lie behind their apparent concern.

121

KING OF CUPS

The king sits on a throne mounted on a stone plinth that lifts him high above the water. He is completely isolated and there is no land in sight. He is staring wearily or perhaps even a little fearfully at his golden cup. This is a strong but sad image. This king rules his kingdom alone, the water surrounding him signifying the world of the emotions. He is also trying to rule his feelings, but to do this he must somehow separate himself from them. He cannot abandon himself to his emotions because the sea of his feelings is so vast that he could ultimately drown in it. Surrounded by so much water that he dare not touch or drink, this king must indeed be thirsty for something. Will he allow himself to drink from the cup that he holds? The King of Cups suggests we apply a huge amount of caution to the way we process our emotions and understand our own needs. Moderation is the keyword here.

Caught between the extremes of his emotional state, the figure here does not know whether to let himself drown in his emotions or pull himself together and try to put these thoughts from his mind. But he has become so introspective that no one feels able to tell him what or what not to do. Although he does not know it he would be

Keywords: moderation, introspection, emotional confusement, diplomacy, wisdom, supportive, reliable, secretive.

wise to seek advice, he has worked so long and hard to keep his own head above water that he is now between the devil and the deep blue sea. His difficulty is in allowing himself to take his own advice and find within himself the dry land that will allow him to feel without fear of drowning.

The King of Cups indicates a person who, on the surface, appears to be in control, and who is seemingly someone we would come to in an hour of need. Their exterior face, however, hides an emotional fragility that may well have been caused by years of denial of their own needs. They have always put themselves last, with the result that they are unable to connect even with themselves on an emotional level, never mind with anyone else. As friends, they will willingly listen to our troubles, but when asked to talk about themselves they are liable to become suddenly evasive and thoroughly embarrassed.

123

The Suit of Pentacles is associated with Earth rather than Heaven, the mundane rather than the spiritual, being concerned with the more down-to-earth considerations of the material world. But there can be no thought of higher things if we are lacking the basic necessities of life, such as food and shelter, and we unfortunately have to work for a living in order to provide for ourselves and our families. The type of person depicted in the suit is therefore practical, sensible and hard-working, in other words the 'salt of the earth'.

Pentacles teaches us the virtues of diligence and hard work through which we can attain the things we need or think we need, which will bring us only temporary satisfaction unless we learn to appreciate and be contented with what we have. By allowing ourselves to become over-concerned with material things we may end up chasing empty objects of desire rather than learning what it means to be truly human. This is why, besides being the coinage by which we buy what we need, the pentacle is also the star etched on its surface, indicating a higher purpose. Once we have learned what true fulfilment is, then we will come to see our possessions as the least important things in our lives, having realized that mere 'things' have no power to make us happy and that the more we get the more we want. Now we understand why we have been feeling so strangely dissatisfied for so long.

When the Two of Pentacles appears in a spread, it signifies vast changes and fluctuations that are making life difficult for us. We are finding it hard to manage our finances, even though there have been warnings of a kind, or even the other elements that affect our material lifestyle. We like to imagine we have everything under control, but in reality uncertainty and a lack of trust are making it hard for us to resolve our problems.

What we need to learn is how to stand apart and make decisions that ultimately help us to 'go with the flow'. At first it would seem that making decisions and going with the flow are likely to cancel one another out. The answer may be to work out what we have, what we want, and where we stand in relation to these problems, while trusting that if we take the appropriate steps the Universe will respond and ultimately help us through. When we can confidently manage the two-fold act of choice and trust, both our material and spiritual needs will be satisfied. Sooner or later we will simply have to change, in that we can't put off making decisions forever, allowing fecklessness to creep in which will lead to an inability to see any project through.

THREE OF PENTACLES

In this card three people are having a conversation in a church, one being an artist, holding a palette, who appears to be taking advice from the others. Three pentacles have been carved in the stone high up on the church wall. The Three of Pentacles signifies the artist's or artisan's mastery of their art or skill, and how they may work towards the achievement of perfection. The church setting also suggests that the work may be of benefit to many people and is not merely a private or personal endeavour.

The Three of Pentacles indicates that we are on the brink of an exciting and creative time that promises to bear fruit, in that we are engaged in some important creative work or commission. It may also indicate that our work would benefit from some outside advice, but we must remember that 'too many cooks spoil the broth' and that it is up to us how the finished work is achieved. To this end, we have learned to weigh the spiritual against the material aspects of ourselves, e.g., respect of our artistic integrity against the reward we are expecting for the finished work.

However, the negative attributes associated with this card include a lack of skill resulting in shoddy workmanship, failing to concentrate on the work in hand, banal ideas, signifying a lack of taste and artistic integrity, and being more concerned with the money to be earned from the job than satisfying the client.

Keywords: skill, craftsmanship, creativity, teamwork, co-operation, material gain.

133

FOUR OF PENTACLES

Here, an oversized green chair with golden legs is set in an ostentatious room. On the chair a relatively small man sits, holding four pentacles pressed tightly to his chest. The indication is that although he may have plenty of money, and has a grand house, his miserliness makes him appear small when contrasted with the generosity of others. The Four of Pentacles indicates one of the dangers of having too much in life, and the temptation to value possessions far above their real worth. If wealth and financial success have led to a miserly or ungenerous attitude, then we have come to believe that there is nothing of value in life apart from money. This attitude is, of course, an expression of extreme attachment to the things of this world and is in the long run extremely unhealthy.

The Four of Pentacles indicates we are overprotective of the things we have and will do anything to keep them safe, equating their very possession with emotional security. Most of us, on occasions, find it hard to give away or let go of the things we have. We also fear that if we fail to keep the people we love on a tight reign we may lose them forever. Refusing to let go, however, only makes it more likely that they will become stifled in the relationship and seek somewhere where they

Keywords: possessive, controlling, stubborn, miserliness, ungenerous, fear of rejection or loss.

can be allowed to breathe. What we need to learn is generosity of spirit and to recognize we are at fault when we impose our wills too heavily on others. We may have allowed ourselves to become paralyzed by the fear of loss, but it is only by giving that was are likely to receive. If we persist in this behaviour we may even end up with the feeling, if I can't have it then no one else can. These fears of loss, abandonment and rejection prevent us from being truly alive, and we will never feel really secure in any situation until we learn to relinquish our grip. No amount of security can ever compensate for the sense of fulfilment that comes from knowing how to relax and enjoy things for what they are rather than what we want them to be.

When the Four of Pentacles appears in a reading, the indication is that the person is trying to control or hold on too tightly to their possessions, job, relationship or family. The problem is that the tighter they hold on, the more likely they are to lose what they've got. Right now, this person would benefit from confronting the fears of loss or rejection that are spoiling their lives and concentrate on seeing the true value in the people around them.

FIVE OF PENTACLES

The Five of Pentacles shows two paupers walking in the snow, the woman a little ahead of the man who is blind and on crutches. Nearby, light is streaming from a church window, although neither seems to be aware of the fact. This is a difficult image: the two have nothing to protect them from the weather, so why don't they shelter inside the church?

Sometimes we become so preoccupied with our troubles that we become blind to the kind of support that may be available. It may not come in the form we want, but it is support nonetheless. No one is approaching the two figures here with a miracle solution, such as a pile of gold to pay off their debts, but there is a place where they could stop for the night and recuperate their strength. By ignoring the presence of the church the two are also refusing to connect with their inner or spiritual strength.

Whether we are experiencing financial loss or the loss of something else of importance to us, if we also lose our connection with our sense of inner strength and, most importantly, our notion of our own self-worth, then we only make our situation worse. Perhaps the figures in the picture feel unable to accept help, in that they feel themselves to be too poor, too dirty, too sick. Here, we are being encouraged to remember that no matter what kind of crisis has befallen us we

Keywords: hardship, spiritual separation, unworthiness, self-neglect, despair, exclusion.

136

When the Six of Pentacles appears in a reading, the person drawing it is being asked to examine their attitude both to giving and to receiving. Although the card indicates that material reward is in the offing, it suggests that we look at how we play power games in

order to get what we want. Are we prepared to give a little only if we feel that the other is worthy, or grateful enough to satisfy our own self-regard? Do we feel so unworthy as to feel compelled to beg for attention, money or whatever else it is that we need? It is important to answer these questionsat this stage, lest we remain stuck in an uncomfortable power game for longer than we would wish.

SEVEN OF PENTACLES

The card shows a young man taking a well-earned rest after working hard on his land. He has his back to us but he appears to be contemplating the fruits of his labour. Is he pleased with the yield or is he thinking that it is a paltry return for all his hard work? Following on from the Six of Pentacles, which indicates financial or material difficulties, the Seven of Pentacles signifies that although we are on the verge of reaping the rewards of our efforts, instead of being elated we are feeling strangely disappointed and can't help wondering if these material gains have been worth the sacrifice. This card suggests plenty, but also a lack of fulfilment. Perhaps we have been working too hard and are feeling guilty that we have sacrificed our family and friends to the needs of work. Not only do our achievements suddenly have a hollow ring to them, but we also have the nagging feeling that we should have been more successful than has turned out to be the case. But fear of failure, when we have already done so much, is a useless emotion at this time. Perhaps this is the time to take a thorough look at our lives, which is usually far from our thoughts when our minds are frantically occupied elsewhere. Are we still on course? Why aren't we getting the results we desire?

Keywords: lack of fulfilment, evaluation, assessment, working too hard, putting work before relationships, setting impossible standards.

In readings, the Seven of Pentacles suggests that time must be taken to satisfy yourself that you are meeting your goals and expectations. It also emphasizes the importance of fulfilment in our lives, which means finding it not only in our work but also in our relationships; this means not neglecting one at the expense of the other. The person who has drawn the card may be thinking that although they have a conscientious attitude to work they have little desire to complete it. This may be because they have set too high a standard for themselves, or have taken on too much, and that unless they can achieve the perfection they desire there is no point in doing the job at all. It is difficult to tell a perfectionist not to be so hard on themselves, but if it is merely a case of under-stimulation then it would be wise to try a new approach by doing something completely different for a while.

EIGHT OF PENTACLES

The man in the picture is thoroughly absorbed in his work, having learned to channel his energies so that they are at their most productive. The Eight of Pentacles symbolizes the impulse to learn and to broaden our horizons by developing new skills. While The Hermit represents the search for inner knowledge, so this card is concerned with the knowledge that allows us to prosper in the material world. It also indicates the need to pay attention to detail in order to gain satisfaction from a job well done. Here we approach our work with love and enthusiasm, having found fulfilment at last. The fact that our talents are being used so productively not only satisfies our spirit but also provides for the material things of life. This is a wonderful time when we are feeling highly motivated to improve every aspect of our lives, including our jobs, our closest relationships and also our inner selves. We should be mindful, however, of becoming so wrapped up in our work that it becomes the be-all and end-all of everything, putting out of kilter the other important aspects of our lives.

The negative aspects to this card are an inappropriate use of energy and skills for unsuitable ends, dishonest dealings in business affairs, and short-term gain at the expense of long-term profit.

Keywords: knowledge, proficiency, diligence, discipline, dedication, attention to detail, perseverance, enthusiasm.

143

NINE OF PENTACLES

Here a woman, clearly a lady of refinement and grace, can be seen taking a leisurely stroll in her garden. The Nine of Pentacles signifies that although the business of life may be important, we don't have to focus on practical matters all the time, but can afford to indulge in the more civilized pursuits, such as art, music, literature and poetry, indicating that there is more to life than accumulating the things that money can buy. The card also indicates discipline and self-control, for although the woman is clearly rich and has no material worries, she is happy and is thankful for her good fortune because she has mastered her baser instincts, allowing her impulses to work for her because they do not rule her. This is therefore a sign of self-reliance, in that she trusts her own ability to handle each and every situation. The woman's strength lies in the fact that she has become one with the beauty with which she has surrounded herself, making her something of a princess in a tower. But she should beware that the beautiful world she has created for herself doesn't prevent her from engaging with other people, their opinions, or even knowing how to deal with their envy. Although she is so seemingly serene, would she be able to maintain this wonderful equilibrium if challenged by others?

Keywords: accomplishment, refinement, independence, cultured, self-sufficient.

The Nine of Pentacles indicates that the person drawing it is reaping the rewards of their own hard work. They know their own worth and are totally self-sufficient, being devoted to enjoying the finer things in life. They are so self-reliant and independent that they appear not to have noticed the lack of other people in their lives.

This may alternatively be a woman who is married to a successful man, who merely wants her as a decorative companion. If this is the case, she is probably very lonely because she is not on an even footing with her husband. While she has everything that money can buy, what good is it to her if no one can relate to her as a friend or equal?

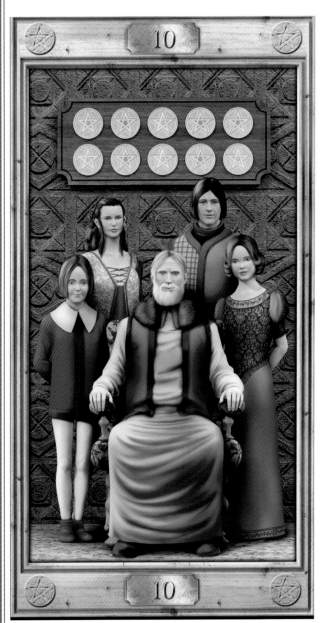

TEN OF PENTACLES

This card symbolizes financial security, accomplishment and comfort, in that the patriarch is now able to rest and enjoy the fruits of his labours in retirement, while he looks on at the lives of his children and grandchildren. Here we see someone who has had a successful career and is now able to rest in the knowledge that what he has created will provide for his family when he is gone. The Ten of Pentacles clearly points to the completion of a cycle. We have learned the lessons of the Nine of Pentacles and rather than the solitary life we have recognized that, for us, a family has more to offer. The framed pentacles on the wall symbolizes security through abundance, but it is interesting to see that they occupy a space where a picture would normally hang. Have we become a little complacent with our lot? Or have we become so focused on the legacy we will be handing down as to lose sight of the people closest to us and their emotional needs? The Ten of Pentacles stands for the ultimate in worldly and material success and is the card you want to see if you are wondering how your latest enterprise will turn out. Wealth and comfort will be yours.

Once material success is ours, we naturally want to preserve what we have. In readings, the card often stands for convention, traditional values and maintaining the status quo, and it may be

Keywords: the good life, wealth, comfort, fulfilment, traditional values, family life, security.

important to trust the established view, because permanence and stability are also indicated here. While some change is unavoidable, the card may be telling you to concentrate on the long-term with an eye to achieving a lasting solution. Now may be the time to settle down and make the arrangements that will work for you far into the future, drawing support and protection from your rich family traditions. By acting conservatively and refusing to take chances, your life is likely to progress on an even keel.

PENTACLES

PAGE OF PENTACLES

The pentacle corresponds to the alchemical element of Earth, and in this sense may symbolize the beginnings of sensual awareness not only in terms of money and its value, but also in a growing awareness of the importance of other physical needs. As indicated by the Page card in every suit, the Page of Pentacles signifies new beginnings, inspiration, and the promise of a creative project or venture in the offing. Here the young man is holding a pentacle very gently between his hands and is staring at it fixedly. He is fascinated by the coin which, to him, seems to promise the fulfilment of all his hopes and dreams – indeed, he is almost overwhelmed by enthusiasm and desire. This is not an indication that his dreams will be realized so much as the initial motivation and energy enabling him to begin the process of bringing them to fruition. This is the card of carefully-laid plans, of 'learning to walk before we run'. If we are able to assess our limitations at the beginning of any new endeavour, and plan each step, then we know we are truly on our way to success. He is now learning to control his day-dreams to combine foresight and practicality in his new venture. The only danger is his tendency to get carried away with his desire for material things, while forgetting the inner or spiritual worth of his intended project.

Keywords: new projects, sense of focus, realistic aims, knowing one's limitations, materialistic, over-optimistic, tendency to day-dream.

When the Page of Pentacles appears in a spread, the person drawing the card is about to begin a time of study or practical preparation for a particular project. The indication is that the person will be a good student, a diligent new employee, and be light-hearted though committed at the start of a new relationship. He or she is patient, but may also lack confidence in themselves or appear somewhat timid. They appreciate and will benefit from the advice of a person with more experience, but they tend to be overly interested in material things, such as money or their appearance. There is still a tendency towards day-dreaming, but this will disappear as the person matures.

KNIGHT OF PENTACLES

The knight, dressed in golden armour, sits astride a black horse that is moving forward at a steady pace. He carries a pentacle in one hand, but unlike the page with his dreamy gaze, the knight looks ahead with a sense of purpose. Here we see the qualities of duty, responsibility and foresight.

Keywords: realistic, hardworking, responsible, inflexible, loath to take chances, warm-hearted, persistent.

This is a person unlikely to rush into anything hastily, but will maintain a pace with which he is comfortable and achieve his goal in an orderly fashion. Here, the usual qualities of action and movement, also exemplified in the other Knights of the Tarot, are grounded, in that he will take care and time over whatever he may pursue in order to secure his success. However, he is also something of a perfectionist, which can often lead him into risking no action at all. The key to this card is patience and generosity. However, we would be wise to be aware that this patience and care of others can sometimes be a cover for indecision and a fear of moving forward in life; without foresight and diligence our projects are likely to fizzle out before they have had a chance to begin.

Whoever draws the Knight of Pentacles in a reading is a warm-hearted and generous person who firmly believes that 'haste makes waste. They will be patient and conscientious, being committed to achieving whatever they set their hearts on but with a job well-done. They believe in being very well-prepared, but this can result in them becoming set in their ways. Such a person will often be particularly resistant, if not absolutely opposed, to unexpected change.

QUEEN OF PENTACLES

The queen sits on her throne which is raised on a stone dais surrounded by grass and trees. She holds up a pentacle, as though it were a mirror, and is gazing into it. This indicates that she understands the value of money and the things that it can buy. Of the four Queens featured in the Tarot the Queen of Pentacles is the most dependable and nurturing. She is the quintessential earth-mother, being sensible and down-to-earth and very much in tune with her own material nature; although she is quite a self-sufficient person, she is a devoted wife and partner to her husband, the King of Pentacles. She is keenly perceptive and able to sum up a situation and is one of those people who is able to 'read between the lines'. Any project she touches involves her whole-heartedly and she is likely to regard it as she would one of her own children. But like most mothers, although she may worry a little that her decisions are just and correct, she invariably trusts her own instincts, which only goes to strengthen her resolve and her faith in her own judgement. Though not intellectual she is a capable and practical women and is an inveterate organizer. She is also creative and resourceful and because she is fond of her own comforts will generously provide harmonious surroundings for everyone else within her circle.

Keywords: earth-mother, nurturing, kind, dependable, sensuous, generous, creative, home-loving.

If taken to the extreme, however, this motherliness can quickly become 'smotherliness'. She may insist on giving too much advice, whether it is asked for or not, and may prevent her children from standing on their own two feet. Another aspect of her character is empathy, in that she is able to put herself in another's place. It is possible that on occasions she is too understanding when a little remonstrance would not go amiss, and she could easily become guilty of killing people with kindness. Sometimes we have to accept that we must be cruel to be kind and allow others to make their own mistakes from which they will hopefully profit.

When this card is drawn it signifies that the person is at one with their surroundings and the people with whom they are involved. They understand how things work and are open-minded and generous. There is a down-to-earth, matter-of-factness about them and because they have a trusting nature others tend to trust them completely. They make good confidants and know how to keep a secret.

MINOR ARCANA

KING OF PENTACLES

Here the king sits on his golden throne, his left hand resting comfortably on the armrest, while the other holds up a golden pentacle. This is a man who is thoroughly at ease ruling over the material world. He is confident and wise, his wisdom coming from the fact that he knows his domain and his people as deeply as he knows himself. He is an excellent provider and is as rich spiritually as he is in the material sense. He takes pride in the fact that he is always right. But beware when this quiet self-assurance suddenly turns to bullying, forcing others to act against their will. Sensuality, wealth and accomplishment are the keys to this card, but be careful not to rest on your laurels or allow yourself to get a little too comfortable!

When the King of Pentacles is drawn the indication is that the person is successful, wise, sensual and well-to-do. They will have reached the top of their profession, helped, no doubt, by the fact that they are born leaders. We can learn a lot from this person and, if we play our cards right, receive a lot from them, whether it be financial or in the form of appropriate advice or connections that will assist us to realize our own desires. This person, however, can be somewhat self-opinionated, and like all of us hates to be shown that he can sometimes make a mistake.

Keywords: successful, wise, a born leader, materialistic, charismatic, no-nonsense attitude, resolute and immovable.

ACE OF SWORDS

The card shows a hand grasping a sword held up to the sky, its tip encircled by a crown with crosses, one for each of the first ten cards of the suit. The Ace of Swords is revealing a new way of thinking, or the cutting away of old habits to make way for a brighter perspective. Like the other Aces in the Tarot, this card points to new energy arising, creating new thoughts, new ideas, new challenges and, because Swords is the suit of truth, new revelations concerning ourselves or others.

The fact that the sword appears out of a cloud suggests these innovations are not yet fully grounded, so that although they are beginning to emerge, they have not yet become fully integrated into our lives. This makes them an exciting but unrealistic prospect, unless we can balance this rush of energy with the dedication required to realize our plans. We will soon be able to capitalize on the energy and determination now becoming available, but failing to act puts us in danger of remaining in the realm of mere ideas and consequently becoming exhausted. Enthusiasm is a great tool, just as long as it is recognized as such and doesn't become an end in itself.

Drawing this card in a reading indicates that the person is on the brink of a great period of renewed enthusiasm, in which they will discover new truths about themselves, their

Keywords: seeing the way forward, new challenges, acting without delay, objectivity, facing reality.

overwhelming sense of loss. Unlike the Two of Swords, which hides itself from the reality of its situation, this card expresses nothing but pain. So how can we escape our sorry plight? Well, perhaps the key lies in the rain/light that falls on the heart. As the heart contracts with pain, the rain falls like tears that wash away the sorrow by teaching us the lesson of acceptance. We may be experiencing the blackness of a storm, but grief itself may show the way through to the other side. If we can only work through our suffering, our hearts may come to feel that love is possible again. It is necessary to have plumbed the depths of our despair before we can

begin to hope; before we know it, we will have come back to life, lighter, braver and wiser than before.

The Three of Swords indicates that a person is in for a heart-breaking experience, making it hard for them to see anything beyond their present pain. This is an experience all of us must go through, at one time or another, and it is indeed part of the human condition to experience these intimations of mortality. We must allow ourselves to grieve for a while, for time heals everything in the end, and we will eventually emerge, stronger than ever, to begin a wiser and more hopeful phase of our lives.

FOUR OF SWORDS

The card shows a stone sepulchre, with four swords hanging on the wall behind it, onto which a person has thrown themselves either in grief or with exhaustion. The Four of Swords signifies withdrawal and shifting the focus inwardly, so that recovery and healing can take place. This period of stillness and introspection is necessary from time to time, and reminds us that we are not invincible but mortal beings who sometimes need to stop what we are doing for a while and accept our physical and emotional limitations. This is not a card of death, but rather an indication that solitude is required, possibly following the painful experiences indicated by the previous card. Despite the fact that we are often urged to seek distractions in order to forget our troubles, it is often of more benefit to us to find a place apart and spend a little time by ourselves, from which we can emerge with our batteries recharged.

The person drawing this card needs to take a break and stand back from their situation. In readings, the Four of Swords is often a sign that we need to slow down and get some rest. If you are recovering from an illness, allow yourself some quiet time for the healing process to take effect. Alternatively, you may be risking overtaxing yourself if you refuse to take a break, even though you may not think you need one at this time.

Keywords: contemplation, introspection, need for relaxation, making time for oneself, taking stock.

168

169

FIVE OF SWORDS

The card shows a contemptuous person collecting the swords that have been thrown down in defeat. The people in retreat are incapable of fighting any more, possibly because what they were fighting for seems suddenly not worthwhile. The Five of Swords represents ambition in a negative sense, in that blindly seeking success, without thinking of the consequences to oneself or others, is ultimately a loss for everyone involved. Here the victor may be realizing he has won a hollow victory, but he is nevertheless taunting his defeated enemies, or may be calling them cowards, daring them to return and fight.

The Five of Swords is about self-interest. We are well aware that we must think of others, yet we continue to put our own survival first. Yet it may seem as if the Universe is conspiring against us and that we can never win no matter how hard we try. Our pride is easily hurt, so how can we proceed? Here it is also important to look at how we have come to this point in the first place. How important is it for us to win, be it a contract, a rise in salary, a house, or someone's heart. This does not only point to loss, but also to a sensation that our pride in ourselves is under attack.

In readings, the Five of Swords is asking us not only to accept defeat, but also to look within and find out how, knowingly or unknowingly, we

Keywords: self-interest, selfishness, winning at all costs, hollow victory, hurt pride.

unwittingly invited this kind of misfortune into our lives? Perhaps we should learn not to talk too much, be so boastful of our resources, or naively expect so much from others?

When the Seven of Swords appears in a reading, the person is is being asked to be more circumspect when dealing with other people. Where might they have been too open, too naïve, or too vain to see that others around them may be looking for excuses to do them harm?

We can't expect the world to be on its best behaviour all the time, but we can ensure that we refrain from giving out signals and presenting the opportunities for others to manipulate and deceive us.

EIGHT OF SWORDS

It is hardly surprising that the lessons taught by the Eight of Swords should follow on the heels of the one before. Here, a young woman stands in a garden, bound with rope and blindfolded. On the other side of the garden wall the trees are bare and the sky appears grey and threatening; but the side where the woman is seems to be more appealing than the bleak landscape on the other side of the wall.

Surrounding the woman are eight swords, that have been stuck into the ground to form a semicircle that suggests imprisonment of sorts. At first glance we may think, oh poor, poor woman, all bound up and alone! But a closer look will reveal that she is not so tightly bound after all, and that the swords are forming only the loosest suggestion of a cage. So why doesn't she simply walk away?

Rather like the Two of Swords, perhaps the interpretation of this card lies with the blindfold. Here the woman's fears and imagination are making things worse than they really are, and if the blindfold were to be removed she would recognize this. In fact, she is in a prison of her own making. The Eight of Swords indicates how we are often assailed by lack of confidence, feeling that the world is out to get us. Fear has rendered

Keywords: vulnerability, feeling trapped and victimized, powerlessness, seeing things as they really are, taking responsibility.

us immobile, so how to escape from this trap? First and foremost we must remove our blindfold and see things as they really are.

But there may be a real need to protect ourselves at this time, and we may be safer with a sword in our hand or at least by raising our guard. Often, when we feel victimized, we wallow in the fact, failing to recognize we may have had a hand in the situation ourselves. We label ourselves a 'victim' and hope that the situation will solve itself. The problem is we could end up waiting forever. There is no sign of a knight in shining armour coming to the recue of the blindfolded woman. She needs to ask someone to unbind her hands when she will be able to remove the blindfold for herself. Without taking responsibility for her own survival she lays herself open to even greater danger.

When the Eight of Swords is drawn, the indication is that the person needs to understand that their own fears and projections are the attackers in this situation, which is not to say that the danger may not be real. But the way to banish fear is to see things as they are and accept that they themselves have the power to change things for the better. No one can break their spirit unless they are given the power to do so. Perhaps they are more afraid of taking a stand than putting up with the status quo, in that the devil we know is sometimes easier to deal with than the devil we don't, but they are more resourceful and stronger than they realize. During this time it is important never to lose sight of this, lest they remain shackled in the prison of their own making. It is only when they grow tired of being the victim that there will be an option for change.

NINE OF SWORDS

This is not an easy card to interpret. Here a woman, seemingly having awoken in the middle of the night, is seen sitting up in bed, her hands covering her face. The simple, almost childish bed presents a strong contrast to the dark wall behind and the nine swords hovering in the air. While it may only have been a nightmare, it obviously feels real enough to the woman.

The Nine of Swords represents mental anguish or self-punishment that includes the fear that a loved one will reject us, die, or leave us for another; the terror of loneliness, ill-health or an isolated old age. This is characterized by sleepless nights, nightmares, together with endless worries indicating guilt, depression and despair, signifying an urgent need for comfort, emotional support, forgiveness and healing.

The card is about real or imagined doubts or pain, just as dreams can be of real or imagined events in our life. It is pointing to a period in our lives when we are being dominated by our worst fears and anxieties. We've probably all had the experience of not being able to sleep because of the negative thoughts we cannot banish from our minds and which seem more intense in the small hours of the night. So what is the lesson of the Nine of Swords? When peace of mind seems a

Keywords: guilty feelings, regret, anxiety, endlessly going over things in one's mind, exerting control over one's emotions.

to be a little immature for his age, having got himself into a situation where he feels a little out of his depth. This person is characterized by the sharpness of their tongue, and there may also be a tendency towards vindictiveness. They are also extremely idealistic, however, and with a lucky star to guide them at this time, their strength and idealism could be enough for them to move mountains!

KNIGHT OF SWORDS

The knight charges forward on his horse, sword drawn, kicking up the dust as he gallops along. In the previous card we saw the Page of Swords, standing and having a good look round. In this, the next stage of development, the Knight of Swords has abandoned his safe vantage point and is moving into the world below. All the Knights in the Tarot are shown on horseback, which suggests that they have learned to harness their powers and drives and use them to achieve their goals, whether they be material, emotional or spiritual.

The Knight of Swords is often taken to represent a confident and articulate young man, who may act impetuously. He knows no limits, and he has all the attributes of bravery, idealism and truth at his disposal; he has also learned how to use them to push forward in his chosen direction. He is the archetypal knight in shining armour, rushing off to achieve his quest head-on. His haste and certainty, however, are also his failings, and he is driving himself and his horse so hard that if he's not careful he will do himself a mischief. When this card appears we would be wise to take full advantage of the energy, idealism and daring suggested by this card, for by being true to ourselves we will accomplish great things. We must remember, however, that this energy is not limitless, nor are we always right in our

Keywords: self-assured, singleminded, impetuous, courageous, self-centred, dynamic, idealistic.

which is what makes him just. He will, if required, use his sword to cut away some of the illusions that are our stumbling blocks, allowing us to see a situation as it really is, whether it be favourable to us or not! The only downside is that by dissecting everything to reveal its core of truth, warmth and emotion has been sacrificed. He has become somewhat controlling and may even be regarded as domineering.

When the King of Swords appears in a reading, all the unnecessary aspects of their situation that are weighing the person down are likely to be cut away. This may or may not be a painful experience, depending on how honest they have been with themselves, but the result should be liberating and bring them directly to their true desires, goals and ambitions. However, this card can also point to situations in which they may feel dominated by the severity of things they are being forced to face, but on no account must they lose faith in ourselves.

This card represents a person who is critical but fair. They are thoroughly connected with the truth and are unhampered by false illusions, although they may have lost some of their warmth of feeling somewhere along the way. They are great leaders, lawyers and businesswomen, but can be controlling and on occasion even abusive.

Wands is the suit of fire, of passion, inspiration and sexuality. Within the suit the cards indicate important discoveries and true progress. They also embody determination, directness and the willpower to see things through. Wands tells us how we should be implementing our bright ideas, where our inspirations lie, and how our passions are affecting our lives. Without that spark of insight we are destined to keep on repeating set patterns of behaviour. Wands ignites something we have forgotten we possessed, such as our long-forgotten dreams and ambitions and, before we know it, we will be irresistibly drawn to acting them out. This is a remarkably creative suit, drawing its strength from the deep reserves of energy that lie dormant within our bodies. The only problem is that unless we rein in the overwhelming enthusiasm likely to be generated, and bring it down to earth, we will only ever have bright ideas and never brilliant results. Thus we are also being taught how to manage our energy, by forcing us to recognize our latent talents and also our limitations. Once we are aware of these, the real work of inner growth can surely begin.

ACE OF WANDS

Here a disembodied hand is offering a large wooden staff or wand, with a few green leaves sprouting from the top of it. The sky is a deep gold and we see mountains in the background waiting to be climbed. The Ace of Wands signifies invention and career opportunities. There is optimism in the air, suggesting we have been given some new and startling impetus to achieve our ambitions. Here, having newly discovered the creative potentiality that has been lying uptapped and neglected within ourselves, we are being offered the wand of inspiration, from which new shoots of potential ideas are already sprouting. Now is the time when we are likely to be struck with that sudden flash of innovative thinking that we can hardly believe came from our own subconscious minds.

It is similar to being given a wonderful gift when the Ace of Wands is drawn during a reading, in that it points the way to a period when new and creative ways of thinking about ourselves, our lives, and the projects within them, may be transformed beyond belief. Here, anything is possible, but if we delay putting our new plans into action this new energy will inevitably dissipate, and we may lose out on the remarkable opportunity being offered to us.

Keywords: creativity, energy, enthusiasm, exciting new career prospects, a widening of perspectives, feeling omnipotent.

The person drawing the Ace of Wands will be experiencing an unexpected rush of physical and creative energy. Some new idea has fired their enthusiasm as never before and they would be wise to take advantage of this certainty and feeling of invincibility that has suddenly visited them. Here the indication is that all things are possible, and they should thank their lucky stars that they are on the verge of a brilliant success. But if they allow procrastination to set in, and fail to grasp the opportunity with both hands, this moment of high energy will quickly desert them and what was once enthusiasm will just as quickly turn to self-doubt. Rare opportunities only present themselves when, by some inner magic that has been performed within us, we are ready to avail ourselves of them. The card suggests that right now we should open the door, vowing never to look back. We may not know where this new opportunity will lead us but the energy to effect this important change has somehow been made miraculously available to us.

The negative side of this card may be an over-confidence leading to recklessness through not adequately thinking through the project in hand.

TWO OF WANDS

A young man stands on the battlements of a great castle, looking out at the spread of the landscape before him. In his left hand he holds a globe of the world and in his right a wand or staff, indicating he is contemplating a journey. To his left side another wand is bolted to the stone wall, possibly indicating he is still in two minds whether to go or stay. The Two of Wands promises much: the youth is looking at the globe, realizing it can give him only the smallest idea of what lies ahead, and he is quite aware that it is the vastness of the unknown lying beyond the horizon that is real. He has long been nurturing a dream, but will it take shape once it is put to the test in the real world? He is understandably a little afraid, but feels that the time has arrived to make this dream a reality at last. What this boy needs is courage. Sometimes we shield ourselves from the dangers of the outside world to such an extent that we prevent ourselves from living our lives to the full, which is the negative aspect of the Two of Wands.

When it appears in a reading, the person drawing the card is leaning towards a direction that inspires them. The idea has not yet been implemented, the danger being that they may spend more time planning and rehearsing their idea than actually getting on with it. It is

Keywords: holding the world in one's hands, originality of thought, seizing the day, taking the initiative.

understandable to be cautious, and wise to think matters through before jumping in at the deep end. All this person needs is to be bolder and more daring, trusting that the time is right to make the creative move of which they have been dreaming for so long. Have courage and be amazed at the results.

THREE OF WANDS

A man stands on a high rock overlooking the sea. He holds one wand in his hand, and there are two others flanking him. He is watching three boats as they sail off into a golden sunrise. He has learned the lesson of the Two of Wands, and instead of remaining safe behind his castle wall, he is confidently acting on his cherished plans, eager to see where they will lead. The Three of Wands therefore represents looking forward to completing a mission with optimism, possibly a commercial enterprise or trade. It is as though each wand is represented by a boat, which is taking our inspiration and invention out into the unknown world. We are happy to watch as our ideas take off, suggesting we have learned to let go and delegate others to fulfil our plans.

Keywords: foresight, expansion, having a mission in life, enterprise, trade, delegating power.

competing energies then we are less likely to get knocked down. Collaboration requires a certain amount of humility, but also a sense of our own self-worth. Here we must be careful to avoid falling into the trap of 'biting off our nose to spite our face' or the kind of attitude that leads us to quit our job before a reason can be found to fire us, or to end a relationship before our partner decides to leave us. Having the courage to fight and to know when to compromise is the key lesson of this card. If we can only recognize our true limitations and learn to work within them we will come through this period relatively unscathed and with a greater understanding and determination to attain what is truly important.

It is only when we are not sure of our capabilities that we can be led into believing we are somehow not good enough or strong enough, or that our ideas are simply too unfeasible to be implemented. With inner knowledge and inner strength our plans and aspirations will survive this testing time and we will emerge with renewed self-respect and a truer understanding of our inner workings.

When the Five of Wands appears in a reading, the person drawing the card is entering a

situation where rivalry and competition will be much in evidence. This may be taking place on an inner level, where different ideas compete for prominence in their minds, threatening to tear them apart, or on an outer level where others are attempting to cut them down to size. At this time they are being taught that if they can only understand what really makes them tick then no one and no thing can convince them they are less than they really are.

SIX OF WANDS

The Six of Wands shows the return in triumph of the victor of a joust, his lance crowned with a wreath of laurel, being applauded by an admiring crowd. But when we look more closely at the horse and its rider we can see that the horse is far too big for him. Although this is plainly a scene of triumph and recognition, there are some aspects of this card that lead us to question how this victory was achieved.

In this deck, it is the lance or wand that bears the victor's crown and not the rider's head, suggesting humility on his part, and that it was participation rather than winning that has been given pride of place. The man is sufficiently in charge of his own ego to allow him success without overweening pride. Moreover, each one of his supporters has a wand of their own, suggesting an element of equality and participation. This is a successful person, well aware of his own worth, who has learned the lessons taught by the Five of Wands, in that to be truly victorious we must allow the people surrounding us a chance to contribute, for we will not make friends if we grab all the credit for ourselves.

A slightly more dangerous aspect of this card, however, is indicated by the fact that the horse's form is almost entirely obscured. Despite the

Keywords: accomplishment, pride, victory, feeling superior, arrogance, condescension, taking all the credit oneself.

man's obvious dedication to the task in hand and to the well-being of those around him, his horse adds a discordant note to this seemingly wonderful story, in

that it is so hidden from view as to lead us to wonder what is going on underneath. Is it really a Thoroughbred? Or has this man ridden to victory while concealing a deception? Moreover, it is the man and his achievement that is being applauded, and not the means by which he was transported to victory. Perhaps, when we achieve a victory, we should be giving more credit to the other people in our lives who have contributed to our moment of triumph, for no one in this world operates in total isolation. Although it is natural to look for personal success, it is necessary to inquire into the means by which our success has been achieved. Have we neglected or sacrificed others in order to win? Although dedication is important in attaining any goal, we must acknowledge that over-achievement is bought only at a price, and that it may be more than we can truly afford to pay.

When the Six of Wands appears in a reading, it indicates that a person can expect recognition because a plan or project has achieved enormous success. They have learned how to work with others to achieve their goal, having put the project and not their own personal reward first, and they have given to others the recognition for their participation that they deserve. But the card also poses some awkward questions: have we used deception in order to win? Have we overtaxed ourselves to the detriment of our own emotional, spiritual or physical well-being? Self-discipline and single-mindedness are necessary tools, but if we've allowed them to get out of control they will clearly degenerate into compulsive behaviour which may well end up taking over our lives.

SEVEN OF WANDS

The card shows a man on higher ground, seemingly defending himself against six approaching enemies. He has been forced to retreat to the edge of the cliff, but he is holding on defiantly, more than ready to meet his foe. An interesting aspect is that the approaching forces are concealed below the bottom edge of the card, leaving only the tops of their cudgels visible. Following the lessons taught by the Six of Wands, perhaps the things that we repressed in order to achieve our victory are now rising from the depths of our unconscious minds, demanding that we deal with them now. Here, our values and our confidence in ourselves, our ideas and plans are what are being threatened. If we give way now we are likely to lose our position on the high ground, and suffer an ignominious end. This is the card of defensiveness and it is time to stand up and fight.

We must be prepared to defend ourselves, but we must also look at our reasons for taking a defensive stance. What deep fears, insecurities or emotions are being stirred by the prospects of a battle? Although we may have received only one clear challenge, the danger has somehow become magnified by the perceived threat to ourselves. The only way to defeat these assailants is by finding what we believe to be true within us and fighting tooth and nail to keep it safe.

Keywords: gaining an advantage, feeling under attack, defensiveness, defiance, protecting all that one has, preserving one's integrity.

can't predict whether all the wands will fall on fertile ground, but the odds certainly look good. This is because we have learned to engage with the act of creativity itself rather than dwell on any misgivings we may have had regarding our endeavours or their outcome. Trust and surrender to forces greater than ourselves provide us with an almost superhuman chance of success.

When the Eight of Wands appears in a reading it is time to get ready to re-energize what may have lost its impetus, using this rush of limitless energy that accompanies the productive or creative part of our endeavours. We have learned to be receptive to new ideas while continuing to focus our willpower towards achieving a result. Although we keep our desired aims fully to the fore, we must prevent them from overshadowing our current state of productivity. In a strange way, this makes us more likely to succeed, and rather sooner than we expect, for we are swept up in the rush of creativity unhampered by extraneous thoughts. We would be wise to remember, however, that despite this excitement we must remember to keep our feet firmly on the ground.

MINOR
ARCANA

NINE OF WANDS

Here an armoured guard is leaning, his eyes half-closed, on a wand. He has made a wall out of the other eight wands which he has set into the top of the existing stone battlements. He seems dejected and lost in thought. The Nine of Wands signifies a situation from which it is often difficult to break loose. The man's defensiveness has nothing to do with his surroundings, but is based on his memories and on the past experiences that have gone to form his character. He is actively engaging with his perceived situation, making sure he's doubly safe, just in case. He may be wise to be doing this. If our naivety or trusting nature has led us in the past into dangerous or difficult situations, when we find ourselves in similar circumstances, we are likely to be overly defensive. It is the concept of 'once bitten, twice shy' that this card exemplifies, and it is easy to understand why it comes after the lesson taught by the Eight of Wands, which equates trust with creativity. The Nine of Wands is saying that we can be prevented from living by something that may have happened to us in our past. We have to find a way to regain confidence in ourselves and our choices so that we can move on and live a full life once more. This may need some work on our part, but we are being asked to look at how our previous mistakes or

Keywords: vulnerability, suspicion of others, going over past hurts, repeating one's mistakes, learning to take each new situation as it comes.

sense of having been victimized are currently holding us back by preventing us from trusting in our instincts. We can start by abandoning the addictive behaviour of endlessly going over past hurts and opening our eyes to the reality and positive energy of living in the present.

When the Nine of Wands appears in a spread, the person drawing the card is experiencing an overly defensive period in their lives. They are unable to see the reality of their situation because they cannot draw a line on memories of past hurts. Here, they need to find a way to trust their own instincts and recognize when real danger exists, so that they are in the best position to prevent themselves from repeating past mistakes. If they have suffered horribly, it may have become part of their mindset that the past will be repeated over and over again. They cannot help remembering how powerless they were made to feel at the time, and are terrified of finding themselves in the same situation again. The trick here is to learn to see things as they really are, recognizing the uniqueness of each new situation rather than allowing it to be clouded by ancient fears. By learning to live in the present, but without throwing all caution to the wind, they will be engaging in a life that is fuller and more authentic, and which will allow their powers of judgement to develop still more.

TEN OF WANDS

The young man holds ten wands in a rather precarious grasp as he strides along the castle ramparts. The wands have begun to fan out in front of his face, obscuring his way forward and making it likely that he will drop his load. This doesn't seem to deter him, however, and he continues to stride confidently forth. Although he is acting in a rather foolhardy manner, he appears to have faith in himself, when it is likely that he has taken on too much alone; but his stubborn pride prevents him from seeking help, and he may even have assumed a load that, in truth, is not his to bear. The key to this card is the notion of responsibility. Whose job is it to do what? Has the man, through pride or self-deception, made himself believe he is the only one capable of doing the job? If this is the only way he can think of to carry his bundle, why has no one suggested a better way?

The Ten of Wands suggests that while we are bravely soldiering on we may have bitten off more than we can in fact chew. This may be laudable in some respects, but we may find ourselves inevitably unequal to the task, lose our way, or become so exhausted as to be unable to finish it, all because we were too proud to ask for help. Consequently, we are feeling trapped, frustrated, overburdened and strangely abandoned. The question we need to ask

Keywords: perfectionist, being too willing to please, life an uphill struggle, feeling put upon, over-burdened, frustrated.

ourselves is, are we overextending ourselves to a dangerous degree?

When the Ten of Wands appears in a reading the indication is that the going seems to be tougher than usual. The person is feeling that life is an uphill struggle and that everything that needs to be done is being left to them. The advice is to be kind to yourself. Lighten the load whenever you can, and allow others to help you, even though you may think you do the job better yourself. You are in fact encouraging others to sit back and watch you work, who will end up unable to do anything for themselves when you finally crack. Forget the high standards you have set yourself which, as time goes by, you will find impossible to maintain alone.

PAGE OF WANDS

The page stands proudly, holding his messenger's wand, his yellow tunic bearing the image of a fiery salamander, symbolizing the enduring faith which triumphs over the fires of passion. Whenever animals are depicted in the Tarot, their purpose is to draw our attention to the fact that our energy, in this case our fiery, creative energy, flows in a circular form. There are no final endings, only endings that point to new beginnings.

The young man has only recently become aware of his own intuitive desires, and doesn't quite know what to do with them yet. He has reached a new level of awareness that leads him to question whether his previous desires were actually his own or in fact belonged to others, and which he was expected to fulfil. Now he has come of age, he sees himself as autonomous and begins to live accordingly.

The Page of Wands indicates we have learned to trust ourselves, in the knowledge of our true desires, allowing us to focus all our energy in one direction, confident that it is the right one for us. When the card is drawn in a reading it signifies a fiery person who may be somewhat self-centred. This is not because they are narcissistic, but because they are consumed by new notions of themselves and of the world around them. This

Keywords: fresh ideas, creativity, intuition, drive, power, desire, lacking in experience but not in enthusiasm, childlike exuberance, charming, unpredictable.

person is committed to understanding themselves and setting a project in motion. They are strong-willed, and their intuitive powers can seem uncannily correct, but they still find it difficult to commit to one project at a time. They are themselves unpredictable, their heads being crowded with too many ideas that jostle with one another for space. But their vulnerability makes them childlike and their natural charm makes it hard for us to remain critical of them for too long.

215

KNIGHT OF WANDS

The knight is galloping at full tilt, his lance held high above his head, his horse's hooves throwing up stones and dust into the air. This man is a risk-taker, but his seeming foolhardiness comes from self-confidence and the ability to judge when it is right to quit or when it is better to forge ahead. Although not every risk taken will turn out for the best, the Knight of Wands teaches that we can't always protect ourselves from danger or failure. Without the confidence in ourselves and our ideas to venture forth, to take risks, to live passionately without fearing what others may think of us, we might just as well stay at home, our blinds drawn, and miss out on ever feeling truly alive. This is a card of spontaneity, joy and daring. But although we would be wise to capitalize on the energy, trust and passion of the knight, we should also remember to be alert to what is going on around us. Heroes are the ones who make it back home after their adventures.

When the Knight of Wands is drawn in a reading, the indication is that the person is dynamic and truly adventurous. They know how to live passionately and their enormous zest for life is likely to be an inspiration to others. But as fast as they appear in someone's life, they will disappear out of it. This person is always seeking a new adventure, having arrived at a place in their lives

Keywords: dynamic, self-confident, risk-taker, zest for life, easily bored.

where to risk danger feels safer to them than the feeling of being suffocated by all that is conventional. Although their enthusiasm is intoxicating, they can on occasion be thoroughly irresponsible. They may act without thinking and are frquently liable to get into hot water due to their fiery temper.

QUEEN OF WANDS

The queen sits on her throne, one hand holding a wand, the other a sunflower. She exemplifies the bright, solar energy that infuses our desires and our creativity. She knows what she wants and, by aligning herself with the solar energy that gives life to all creation, she usually gets it. It was once thought that Earth was the centre of the Universe, but we now know that Earth orbits the Sun and not the other way around. The Queen of Wands indicates we must be open and flexible enough to place our creative energy at the centre of her Universe, in that she sees herself as its conduit. This is the secret of her almost magical power to imagine, create and see her projects through. As soon as we lose sight of this thought, we become self-centred and in danger of losing our connectedness with this phenomenal creative power.

When the Queen of Wands represents a person in a reading, it follows that they are highly creative, but that their creativity is matched with a shrewd ability to get things done in the world. This person never takes no for an answer, but rather than bending you to their will, they will somehow inspire you to adopt their cause. This person is dynamic, exciting and deeply committed to whatever they do. But we must first learn how to approach them and how to stand our ground, lest we be consumed by the flames of their superabundant energy

Keywords: imperious, magnetic, passionate, powerful, inspirational, dynamic.

KING OF WANDS

The King of Wands sits a little uneasily on his throne, dressed in red and black. The emblem of the salamander is on his breast, biting its own tail and symbolizing infinity. The king is the master of the world of fire, making him creative, passionate and jealous. He has been born to lead but does not necessarily enjoy taking responsibility, but he nevertheless exudes energy, excitement and confidence, being the person to whom people are naturally attracted and who will follow his lead. The King of Wands indicates someone persuasive enough to get others to do their work for them because, although they are the initial creative impetus, their enthusiasm soon wanes, and the drudgery involved in realizing their project suddenly seems too much like hard work.

When the card represents a person in a reading, they are likely to be inspiring and with noble aims. They are captivating people who understand our ideas or projects and how to realize them. However, they are overworked and their enthusiasm may be suffocated under the weight of their responsibility to others. They are the passionate magicians who, at the end of the day, find it difficult to act consistently, even though they may not show it, for beneath their drive, enthusiasm and business acumen, they are liable to slip away and dream about the holiday they are

Keywords: powerful, vital, energetic, enthusiastic, confident, persuasive, inconsistent.

never likely to permit themselves to enjoy. Although they may be charismatic and charming, such people should never be taken seriously, for anyone who does so is liable, emotionally, to get their fingers burned.

NOW LET'S LOOK AT THE POTENTIALS.

In order to move ahead in his academic career, F could do with learning how to intuit what would be most enjoyable for him rather than always focusing on what is the best route out of one project and into the next. The Four of Wands is a card of celebration and joy. Instead of intuiting that if he soberly sets his sights on his goal, and doesn't waver, he will achieve it, what actually might be better for him is to relax a little and understand that if he learns how to be satisfied with his present situation and live it to the full, he is more likely to open pathways that are more suitable for him in the long run.

The next card further underlines this. In the 'feeling' section (position six), F has chosen the Four of Pentacles. This suggests that becoming aware of how his need for security is stifling his opportunity for growth is of utmost importance. If he can only learn to let go, he will be much better off for it in the future.

The next card, the Ten of Wands, appears in the 'thinking' section and points to overexertion in this area. F has so many projects and ideas in the pipeline that, again, the best potential for him is to let go of a few of them and concentrate on one or two for the time being. If he can do this, he's more likely to succeed. I assure him that he doesn't have to let go of all his ideas forever, but that right now it's better for him to prioritize.

Lastly, we get to The Hanged Man (position eight). Once again, the Tarot tells us that F needs to sacrifice something in order to get what he wants in the long run. He needs actively to let go of things and change the perspective of his career path in order to succeed. Being a man of many options, he squirms a little when I tell him this, so we then proceed to the final lesson card.

The lesson F has chosen is the Two of Swords, which makes perfect sense, in that it indicates F's tendency to retreat from making choices. When options present themselves he becomes afraid of making the wrong choice and so opts to make no choice at all, keeping everything up in the air. This makes him vulnerable, so it is no surprise that he should feel threatened by colleagues or competitors at work (see position two). In fact, he never stays long enough in one place to establish himself in his position.

Ultimately, F needs to learn that choosing or prioritizing his efforts will lead to greater success in his career (The Hanged Man/Ten of Wands/Two of Swords). He will also profit from being less hard on himself (Six of Swords) and will benefit from learning how to enjoy what he's got (Four of Wands). If he can do this, then he stands a better chance of relaxing his grip (Four of Pentacles) and will stand to gain more in the long run.

When I survey all the cards he's drawn, I come back to the Ace of Pentacles next to the Ace of Cups. I get the idea from these two cards that there's a further dimension to the problem. I ask him how he's balancing the needs of his career and his home life. He tells me he's recently married and that he and his wife are thinking of having a child, but neither he nor his wife are sure if it's the right time in terms of their careers. Seeing the Four of Wands and the Ace of Cups I ask him to imagine what he would most like in life if the stress of his drive to achieve was absent from the equation. I ask him not to tell me, but to work this out for himself and then choose whatever the answer is as his next most important move at this time. I reiterate the importance of the lesson that teaches him to make choices, rather than sitting on the fence, and then bring the reading to a close. The reason I do this is to encourage F to think for himself; after all, that's what his lesson is, the Two of Swords suggesting his need to have the courage of his own convictions.

For a quick potentials reading you can always use a simple two-card spread. The first card indicates how things are currently and how they are likely to change in the not-too-distant future. For example:

A client wants to know how his financial situation will turn out. I ask him to shuffle the cards, then fan them out in front of him. He chooses one card for now and one for the potential future change.

SAMPLE READING:

Now   *Future change*

I suggest his finances are unstable and somewhat up in the air. He seems to be in the process of juggling money around in order to make ends meet, and has to beware of getting into debt. However, something is coming along that will bring this unstable period to an end. A large sum of money, either from an institution or an inheritance, seems to be coming his way. Is he expecting money from a family source? The client confirms that although his father died a long time ago, he has been waiting for an old legal issue, to do with money owed to his father, to be resolved. If the results are favourable, he stands to gain a large sum of money.

The next type we can look at is a spread about relationships, which I developed some years ago to look at the factors that went into making up a marriage or partnership. The spread focuses on how the two people are relating to each other and what it is that they have in common that highlights the strengths and weaknesses of their relationship. Once these are identified, it becomes easier for them to see what they might want to change.

The first eight cards are divided into two columns *(see right)*.

A further ninth card is chosen to show what the two have in common and so figure out the best ways of working things out or improving the relationship. Supplementary cards can be chosen, after the initial nine, to answer further questions, such as, where is it likely to go from here?

Sample Reading:

M was single at the time of the reading and wanted to know what the potential was for a future relationship. I asked her to shuffle the cards while thinking about herself in conjunction with her intended new partner. I fanned out the cards in front of her and she chose the following *(see page 234)*:

Let's look at M first. In terms of a potential relationship she seems to be wondering if she might be biting off more than she can chew. She has much to consider yet seems to be determined to do things her way and without relying on outside advice. In terms of her emotions, however, she is likely to fall head-over-heels for this man and must guard against infatuation. Her actions are likely to involve risky behaviour which, to others, might appear foolish in the extreme.

The striking thing about M's cards is that they strongly indicate a woman who may already be the classic archetype of the foolish and besotted lover. The headstrong Ten of Wands, acting out the risk-taking, independent fool, indicates she is being emotionally driven by a feeling of overwhelming love for

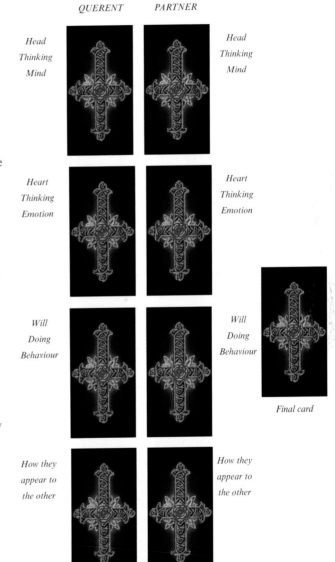

QUERENT   PARTNER

*Head
Thinking
Mind*

*Head
Thinking
Mind*

*Heart
Thinking
Emotion*

*Heart
Thinking
Emotion*

*Will
Doing
Behaviour*

*Will
Doing
Behaviour*

Final card

*How they
appear to
the other*

*How they
appear to
the other*

stand her in good stead while performing, or re-engaging with the world.

Then looking again at the first six cards, culminating in The Hermit, I noticed that they all featured lone characters, none of whom appeared to be in the least bit lonely. I mentioned

this to her, and she replied that she had been feeling rather isolated and was concerned to hear that she was in for more of the same (The Hermit). I again drew her attention to the Empress crossed with Strength, telling her that most women I knew would be more than delighted to draw these two cards and in these positions, and that she had no reason to feel sorry for herself.

Her strong self-awareness was then demonstrated in the Page of Swords (position seven). I suggested she might currently be developing her own independent thoughts and ideas, but was very aware of criticism and even attack, which was making her guarded and mistrustful of the people

around her. Given the six previous cards, I ventured the opinion that this was not a bad stance to take, and that she had clearly achieved a lot following her decision to withdraw for a time.

The next card, showing outside forces, or how P appeared to others, was the Page of Wands (position eight). Again this suggested independence, but whereas the previous card signified independence of thought, the Page of Wands indicated

bright new inspirations and passions coming her way. This card, however, in combination with the first two cards of the spread, suggested a discrepancy between how people saw her and how she really was. The first two cards showed her to be a mature and independent woman, whereas others might be seeing her as young for her age and a little immature. Remembering how she had mentioned her family earlier, I wondered if this might be their opinion of her.

In the position of hopes and fears she had drawn The Emperor (position nine), which indicated she was hoping to stabilize her life and make her plans more concrete and workable. But it also indicated a fear of being controlled.

Lastly, the final conclusion to all of these different aspects of her present life came up as the Ace of Wands (position ten), signifying she would emerge from this period invigorated and with new plans, passions and directions. As long as she persevered in realizing her hopes and making her plans workable (The Emperor), she was likely to go far in her chosen direction.

It's interesting to make a few further observations at this point. The first six cards of the reading are generally related to the client's inner world, whereas the remaining four are to do with how they appear to the outer world. P was, in fact, much stronger on the inside than she appeared on the outside. Why? The answers, in this particular reading,

lie in positions seven and nine: position seven indicates P has a profound mistrust of the world, and but for having The Empress crossed with Strength at the centre of the spread, might have pointed to an over-anxious or even paranoid personality. The negative side of the card in position nine (The Emperor), is control. Perhaps an overwhelming fear of being controlled was preventing P from making any firm commitments to her projects difficult. Luckily for P, however, she was about to enter a stage, characterized by The Hermit, suggesting wisdom and acting on sound advice.

In this reading, both The Empress and The Emperor appear along with the Page of Swords and the Page of Wands. P confirmed she was the middle child of three siblings. The Nine of Pentacles, along with the Ace of Wands, suggested she had found her independence and was about to break previous bonds and start living her own life, the powerful cross-combination of positions one and two indicating inner triumph and abundance.

Although the Celtic Cross is one of the more popular spreads,

using it a few times may lead you to create different spreads of your own. This is probably the best way to proceed, for they will make more sense to you than anyone else's, and are guaranteed to make all your readings totally unique to you.

12 LE PENDV

13

19 LE SOLEIL

14 LA TEMPERANCE

15 LE DIABLE

16 LA MAISON-DIEV

18 LA LVNE

17 LES ETOILES

5 LE PAPE

4 L'EMPEREVR 7

6 L'AMOVREVX 1

7 LE CHARIOT

ACKNOWLEDGEMENTS

The Publisher would like to thank © Lo Scarabeo S.r.l for supplying the Pictorial Key pack used to illustrate this book.

© Art Directors and TRIP Photo Library pages 47 right, 49, 51 right, 57 right, 75 left: © Art Media/HIP/TopFoto; page 137: © The British Library/HIP/Top-Foto; page 119: © Caro/Topfoto; page 224 left: © Caro/Aufschlager/TopFoto; pages 150 right, 169: © Caro/Bastian/TopFoto; page 209: © Caro/Hoffman/Top-Foto; page 111:© Caro/Oberhauser/TopFoto; page 163, 177: © Charles Walker/TopFoto; pages 16 both, 22, 23, 24, 28 left, 29 left, 32, 73 right, 160, 161, 237 left, 248 all, 252-253, 254-256 all: © Classic Stock/TopFoto; page 103, 115, 129, 165, 205, 219: © E&E Images/HIP/TopFoto; page 67 below right: © The Image Works/TopFoto; pages 55 below, 65 right, 79 top, 105 below, 121, 149 left, 195: © John Hedgecoe/Topfoto; pages 203, 213: © John Powell/TopFoto; page 101, 135, 185, 211: © Kike Calvo/TopFoto; page 171: © Nano Calvo/TopFoto; pages 100, 109: © National Pictures/TopFoto; 131: © Phil Seale/TopFoto; page 81 right: © Photo New Zealand/TopFoto; pages 79 below, 107, 123, 141, 143, 153, 167, 181, 189, 197, 199, 217: © Photri/TopFoto; page 147: © Professional Sport/TopFoto; page 113:© Ria Novosti/Topfoto; page 59: © Regency House Publishing Ltd. with Lo Scarabeo S.r.l.; pages 1, 2-3, 4-5, 6-7, 8-9, 10-11, 12-13, 14-15, 17, 18, 19 left, 20-21, 26-27, 30-31, 33, 34-35, 36, 37, 38, 39, 40-41, 42, 43, 44, 45, 46, 47 left, 48, 50, 51 left, 52, 53, 54, 56, 57 left, 58, 60, 61, 62, 63 below, 64, 65 left, 66, 67 top and left, 68, 69, 70, 71, 72, 73 left, 74, 76, 77 left, 78, 80, 81 left, 82, 83, 84, 85, 86, 87, 89, 90, 91, 92-93, 94-95, 96, 98, 99 top, 102, 104, 105 top, 106, 108, 110, 112, 114, 116, 118, 119 left, 120 left, 122, 124, 125, 126-127, 128 left, 130, 132, 134, 136, 138, 139 right, 140, 142, 144, 145 left, 146, 148, 149 right, 150, 152, 153, 154, 156-157, 158-159, 162, 164, 165 left, 166 left, 168, 170, 172, 174, 176, 178, 180, 182, 184, 185 left, 186, 188 left, 190-191, 192-193, 194, 196, 198, 200, 202, 204, 206, 208, 210, 212, 214, 215 right, 216, 218, 220, 222-223, 225, 226-227, 228-229, 230-231 232-233, 234-235, 236, 237, 238-239, 240, 241, 242-243: © TopFoto; pages 55 top left, 117, 155: © TopFoto/Caro; pages 99 below, 188 right: © TopFoto/Fortean; page 251: © TopFoto/Fotomas; pages 19 right, 25: ©TopFoto/Keystone; page 175, 183: © TopFoto/Langhurst; page 133: © Topham/PA; page 207: © Topham/Photri/TopFoto; page 151, 201, 221: © Topham Picturepoint/TopFoto pages 29 right, 63 top, 75, 77 right: © TopFoto/Powell TopFoto; page 120 right, 166 right/215 left: © Ullsteinbild/Top-Foto; page 97, 128 right, 139 left, 145, 179, 187, 224 right:

NOTES